# Entertainment Centers You Can Make

Also by Paul Gerhards

*Garden Structures You Can Make*
*Backyard Play Areas You Can Make*
*Children's Furniture You Can Make*
*How to Sell What You Make*

# ▪ Entertainment Centers You Can Make ▪

## Paul Gerhards

STACKPOLE
BOOKS

Published by
STACKPOLE BOOKS
5067 Ritter Road
Mechanicsburg, PA 17055

Printed in the United States of America

10 9 8 7 6 5

FIRST EDITION

Cover design by Caroline M. Stover
Cover photo by Paul Gerhards

**Library of Congress Cataloging-in-Publication Data**

Gerhards, Paul.
    Entertainment centers you can make / Paul Gerhards.
    —1st ed.
        p.    cm.
    ISBN 0-8117-2746-7
    1. Entertainment centers (Cabinetwork)    2. Built-in furniture.    I. Title
TT197.5.E5G47    1997
684.1'6—dc21                                        97-107
                                                        CIP

# ▪ Contents ▪

# ▪ Introduction ▪

The concept of home entertainment likely began the day Dad unpacked that new Victrola, cranked it up, placed a chunky slate disk on the turntable, and then stood proudly by as the family marveled at the sweet strains of Enrico Caruso.

Thomas Edison's invention was followed by the drama of radio with "The Shadow," the spectacle of television with Ed Sullivan, and the trumpeting of hi-fi with Louis ("Satchmo") Armstrong.

Today, with compact disks, videocassette recorders, Dolby stereo, and satellites beaming signals to televisions the size of small cars, home entertainment is big business. Indeed, the focal point of many living rooms and family rooms is the TV.

Along with these forms of home entertainment came a need for some way to organize and store all the gizmos, gadgets, and odds and ends. The entertainment center, that piece of furniture holding it all together, fills the bill.

Building your own entertainment center allows you to suit your particular needs. Your entertainment center can be simple or complex, depending on your woodworking skills and your desires. You also get the reward of showcasing your efforts—this furniture is, after all, a centerpiece for all to see.

With this book I take a "kitchen-cabinet" approach to building entertainment centers. Just as a kitchen can be fitted with cabinets of standard dimensions arranged to suit the shape of the kitchen and the needs of those who use it, so, too, can an entertainment center be built by assembling smaller components into a larger whole. Contained in the book are plans for a dozen cabinets that can be assembled in seemingly limitless arrangements. In addition, I suggest different ways you can vary the style of your entertainment center to help it fit with your decor.

In Part I of the book are brief discussions of some of the materials you'll use, examples of basic joinery, and a few notes on finishing.

Part II focuses on planning and building your entertainment center. There you'll find detailed drawings of the modules you'll use to build the unit you want. I also offer options that add versatility to a given entertainment center. While looking at the drawings, keep in mind that the plans are not absolute. Think of them rather as a collection of ideas, a springboard for your imagination.

# Part I: The Basics

---
## ▪ Chapter 1 ▪
---

# MATERIALS

## SOLID STOCK

The term solid stock refers to lumber milled directly from logs. This distinguishes it from composite forestry products such as plywood and reconstituted products such as particle board. Lumber products are sold in various dimensions and stages of finish, from rough sawn to S4S—meaning surfaced four sides—depending on their intended end use. Solid stock can be either hardwood, cut from deciduous trees, or softwood, cut from coniferous trees. Some "softwoods," however, are harder than some hardwoods. Most furniture is made of hardwood, but some softwood is also used. Eastern white pine is a good example. And it's not uncommon to find a variety of woods in a single piece of furniture, either for visual effect or to substitute a less costly piece of wood where it won't be seen. What kind of wood you use to build your entertainment center will depend on personal preference, cost, and availability.

Most of us are familiar with such lumberyard terminology as 2×4 and 1×12. Wood sold in lumberyards is primarily softwood and used for construction. Lumber is milled in uniform increments of length, width, and thickness. These products are sold at retail by the linear foot.

In most cases, hardwood is priced and sold by the board foot (cubic foot). Figure 1.1 shows the formula for calculating board feet.

Also shown are the board-foot equivalents of 1 linear foot of several 1-inch boards.

Thickness is usually expressed in quarters of an inch, and it refers to the rough-cut thickness of the board. For example, a 4/4 (pronounced four-quarter) board is 1 inch thick, and a 5/4 (five-quarter) board is 1¼ inches thick. Once these boards are sur-

$$BF = \frac{T \times W}{12} \times LF$$

one LF of
| | |
|---|---|
| 1 x 1 | .08 |
| 1 x 2 | .16 |
| 1 x 4 | .33 |
| 1 x 6 | = .50 | BF
| 1 x 8 | .66 |
| 1 x 18 | .83 |
| 1 x 12 | 1.00 |

Figure 1.1. Formula for calculating board feet, where *T* equals a board's thickness, *W* its width, and *LF* its length in feet. When calculating board feet, use the nominal—not actual—thickness. Also shown are the board-foot equivalents of 1 linear foot of seven different 1-inch boards.

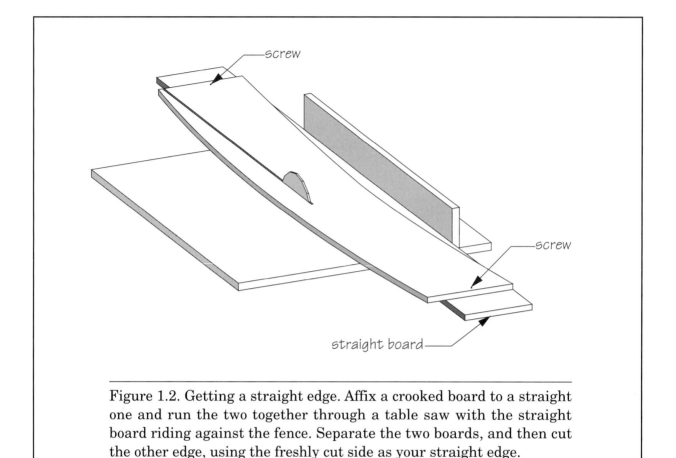

Figure 1.2. Getting a straight edge. Affix a crooked board to a straight one and run the two together through a table saw with the straight board riding against the fence. Separate the two boards, and then cut the other edge, using the freshly cut side as your straight edge.

faced—planed smooth—on their two faces (S2S), they are 13/16 inch and 11/16 inches thick, respectively. Keep in mind, however, that the lumber is priced at the full rough-cut thickness.

Note that even though S2S boards are 13/16 inch thick, the plans call for 3/4-inch boards. This extra 1/16 inch can be used as is or planed off by the woodworker with a thickness planer. If used as is, remember to take this into consideration.

Hardwood dealers often stock thinner boards of the same species, but these 1/2- or 1/4-inch boards are sold by the square foot and typically cost at least as much as the 4/4 stock from which they were milled.

Nearly all solid hardwood lumber used for furniture making and other woodworking projects is S2S and in random widths and lengths. Not only are the edges left rough, but the boards are often crooked as well. This presents a problem for the woodworker, who needs straight edges to work from. Figure 1.2 shows two means of getting a straight edge on a rough-edged board. Avoid boards that are bowed, cupped, or twisted. These are much harder to salvage.

You can request that your lumber be surfaced on one edge (S2S1E or S3S) or milled to any other specification of your choice. Expect to pay a setup charge and an hourly shop rate for these services.

## SHEET STOCK

Although a woodworking purist might build his entire entertainment center out of solid wood, the rest of us would make good use of hardwood plywood or veneered, medium-density fiberboard (MDF). These two materials have the same uses; any reference to plywood in Part II of the book is also a reference to MDF.

Each has its advantages and disadvantages. Plywood is made up of an uneven number of plies (layers), with the grain of adjoining plies running at right angles to each other. This gives a sheet of plywood considerable strength and makes it dimensionally stable. That is, it won't expand and contract with changes in humidity as solid wood will.

A drawback to using plywood is that it may have voids (knotholes and splits) in the core plies. Voids in the wrong place can cause all kinds of problems. In general, the more plies there are, the less likely you'll have trouble with voids. It's possible to obtain plywood that is free of voids, but the price will be higher.

Hardwood plywood is graded with an alphanumeric system, with a letter given to the face and a number to the back. For example, A-1 will have two good sides, with the face being the better of the two. You would use one of these panels where both sides would show, as in the side of a television cabinet. A panel marked A4 would be useful on pieces where only the A side would show, as in a cabinet back.

Like plywood, medium-density fiberboard is dimensionally stable. MDF, however, has the advantages of being void-free and cheaper. MDF is made from individual wood fibers bonded with resin under heat and pressure to densities ranging from 31 to 55 pounds per cubic foot. This density gives MDF its excellent sound-damping quality, which makes the product perfect for building speaker enclosures.

It is this density, however, that leads to the major disadvantage of using MDF. One $3/4$-inch, 4-by-8-foot sheet can weigh as much as 110 pounds, whereas a sheet of oak plywood is only 75 pounds. Consider this factor when planning a large piece of furniture.

One final note about hardwood plywood and veneered MDF. Whereas a $3/4$-inch sheet of MDF is actually $3/4$ inch thick, a sheet of $3/4$-inch plywood is actually $23/32$ inch thick ($1/32$ inch thinner). Although this has little impact in the overall dimensions of a piece of furniture, it does have an impact on joinery, especially if a piece of plywood is intended to fit snugly into a dado cut with a router. Undersized router bits are available for this purpose. A listing of mail-order houses and other establishments of interest to woodworkers is in the Appendix.

# ▪ Chapter 2 ▪

# JOINERY

One of the beautiful things about making your own furniture is that you can make it to your own standards. You choose the materials and how to put them together. It is the putting together that engenders the most pride in woodworking. Joinery is the art and craft of putting boards together in a pleasing fashion, where each joint is either not at all noticeable or noticeable to the extent that it is part of the design.

Like any craft, woodworking takes a good deal of practice and a lot of patience. Patience and skill aside, the two most important aspects of furniture making are using good materials and good tools.

Accuracy in measuring and cutting cannot be overemphasized. Saw blades and other cutting tools should be sharp. Always buy the best tools you can afford. Power tools should run smoothly. Fences should be firm and true to their blades. If possible, avoid power tools with sleeve bearings. This is especially true for circular saws and routers. When shopping for a circular saw (table saw, radial arm saw, or power miter saw), check for blade runout. Grab the blade firmly between thumb and forefinger and try to move the blade from side to side. Any side-to-side movement will show up in your cuts, and accuracy will go out the window.

There is no single best way to approach any woodworking project, and certainly there are as many ways to build something as there are woodworkers. We all have our own ideas, and at the same time, we're always learning ways to do things differently. Dozens of books have been written on how to make good joints, and hundreds of magazine articles have been written on how to do one thing or another better, faster, and more easily. I'm assuming that you have some familiarity with power tools and how to use them, but I am including a few words about some of the more common cuts and joints and procedures that will be useful for building your entertainment center.

## FACE-FRAME AND EUROPEAN-STYLE CONSTRUCTION

As the name implies, a face frame is a framework of solid wood that is applied to the front of a cabinet. When the cabinet proper is made of plywood or MDF, the edges—for the most part—are thus concealed by the face frame. Figure 2.1 shows the components of a face frame.

In European-style cabinet construction, no face frames are used. All facing edges are banded (discussed below). Also, there are lines of door and drawer hardware designed specifically for this method. Euro-style construction has become quite popular in this country, especially for kitchen cabinets. As there are no rails and stiles, the use of solid wood in the cabinet is reduced.

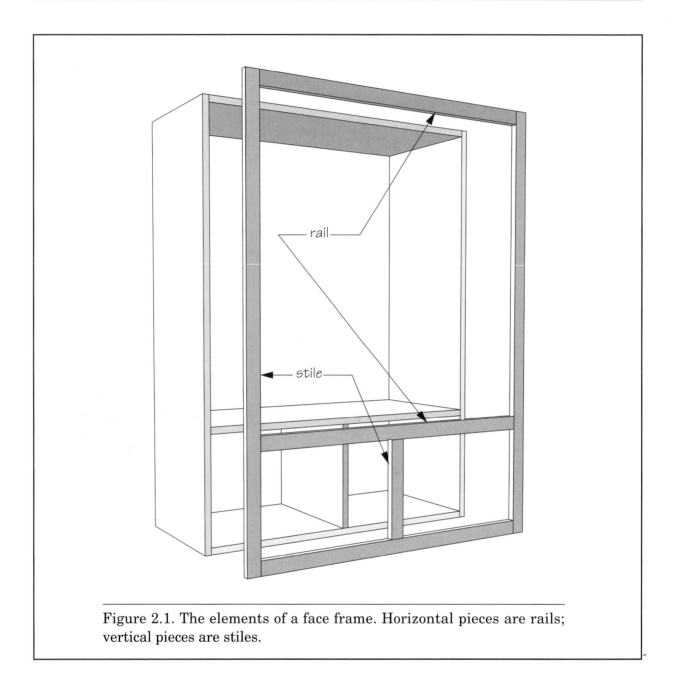

Figure 2.1. The elements of a face frame. Horizontal pieces are rails; vertical pieces are stiles.

With Euro-style construction, doors and drawers provide the visual continuity across a bank of cabinets. A face frame provides a backdrop for doors and drawers and helps tie multiple units together. What's more, a face frame can be dressed up—chamfered (beveled), rounded over, or beaded—thereby adding its own visual interest.

All the components for the entertainment centers described here are of face-frame construction. Adjustable shelves and other members not covered by the face frame will require edging.

## Edge Banding

Edge banding is a method of covering exposed edges of plywood or MDF cabinet members. Edging material is a wood veneer product that comes in rolls. Several different species of wood are available, and there are three different methods of application. Material with a preapplied hot-melt glue is ironed on. You can also obtain the veneer with a pressure-sensitive backing. Last, and most economical, is veneer without any preapplied adhesive. You would use either contact cement or wood glue to adhere the strips. Once the banding is trimmed and lightly sanded, a glue line is virtually indistinguishable. You can, of course, make your own edging by ripping thin strips from stock you're working with.

## Biscuit Joinery

In lower-quality cabinet and furniture making, face frames are nailed together and nailed to the cabinet proper. The use of air-driven nailers makes this process easy and

fast. But relying too heavily on nails detracts from the woodworking experience and is not very aesthetically pleasing. All those nail holes must be filled, and they are never quite invisible.

Biscuit joinery, also called plate joinery, is also easy and relatively fast. It's not as fussy as making mortise and tenon joints and has all but eliminated doweling as a means of joining boards. It leaves no hint of how the boards were joined, but the joints are exceptionally strong.

This method makes use of small, oval biscuits of pressed hardwood that fit snugly into slots cut into each piece being joined (Figure 2.2). Glue is brushed into the slots and along the faces of the members to be joined, and the joint is clamped. The glue

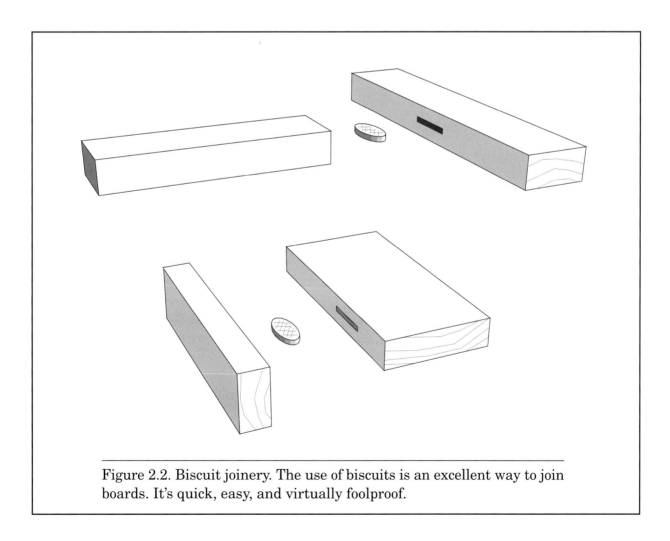

Figure 2.2. Biscuit joinery. The use of biscuits is an excellent way to join boards. It's quick, easy, and virtually foolproof.

causes the biscuits to swell slightly to create an excellent bond.

Biscuits come in three sizes: 0, 10, and 20, with 0 being the smallest. Biscuit joinery requires a special tool, called a plate joiner, for cutting the slots. Expect to pay as much as $150 for this tool. Craftsman, however, makes a suitable attachment for its routers for much less.

A standard joiner cuts slots in opposing pieces at exactly the same distance from the face of each piece, so that alignment is automatic. The only limitation to biscuit joinery is the size of the 0 biscuit. It's $1^7/_8$ inches long, and its slot is slightly longer. This precludes cutting a slot in the end of a piece less than about $2^1/_8$ inches wide.

New on the market is a detail biscuit joiner by Ryobi, which cuts slots for a smaller set of biscuits—sizes 1, 2, and 3—which are $5/_8$, $3/_4$, and 1 inch long.

## Stub Tenon

The projecting piece known as a stub tenon, along with its complementary cavity, called a mortise, is shown in Figure 2.3. These work well in joining rails and stiles of the face frame. For most applications, tenons $1/_4$ inch long are sufficient. Cut the tenons on a table saw or table-mounted router. The mortises are cut with the same router setup. Alternatively, you can cut the mortises by hand, boring out the waste with a drill and finishing up with a chisel.

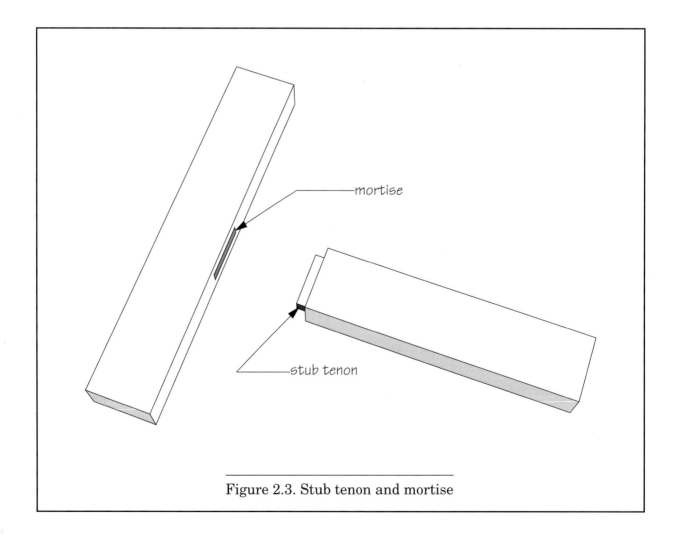

Figure 2.3. Stub tenon and mortise

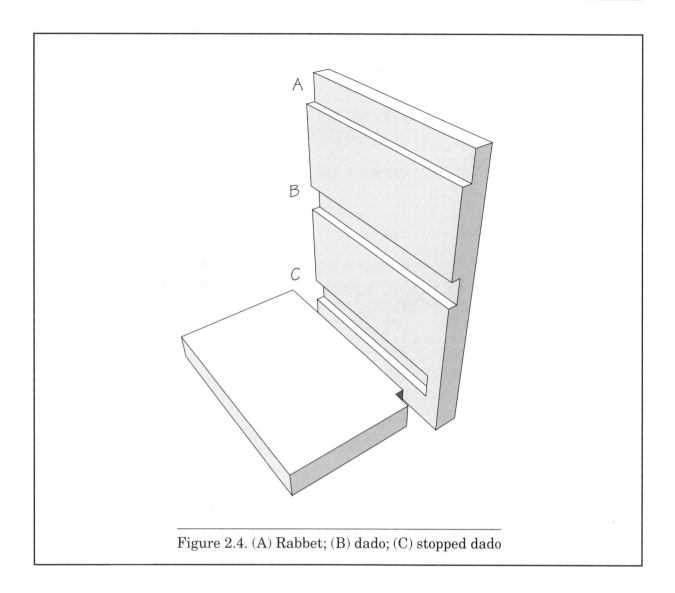

Figure 2.4. (A) Rabbet; (B) dado; (C) stopped dado

## Rabbets and Dadoes

A rabbet cut, shown in Figure 2.4A, is a recess made on any edge of a board. Its typical function is to receive a panel, such as a cabinet back.

Figure 2.4B illustrates a dado cut. These rectangular grooves are typically cut across the grain. A similar cut made with the grain is a plow cut or, if narrower than 3/4 inch, a groove. A dado might receive a fixed shelf or cabinet bottom. Dadoes are also used in drawer construction.

A stopped dado (Figure 2.4C) is one that doesn't run all the way through a piece. This cut is usually used for a fixed shelf where you don't want the joint to show.

## Edge Joint

It's often necessary to join two or more narrow pieces of solid stock together to make a wider board. You would use an edge joint any time a wide board is called for but a piece of sheet stock won't do.

Edge preparation is important to achieve a good joint. The edges should be clean and smooth. Do not, however, use sandpaper to smooth an edge. Rather, edges should be machined with a power jointer. A table saw

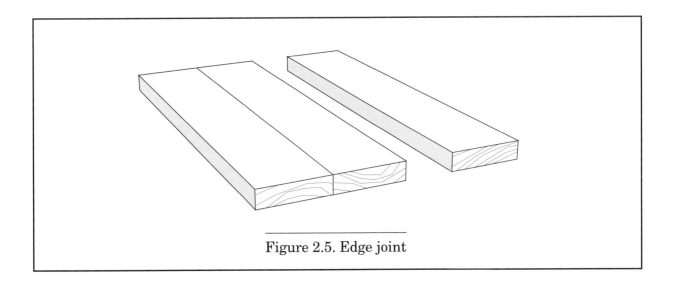

Figure 2.5. Edge joint

or radial-arm saw equipped with a carbide planer blade also produces good results. Of course, you can use a hand-driven jointer plane, but this takes more time. Check to make sure that the mating edges fit evenly along the length of the joint.

When possible, join the boards with the curves of their annual growth rings going in opposite directions, as shown in Figure 2.5. This will help keep the final product flat.

As a rule, no individual solid board should be wider than eight times its thickness. To help prevent a wide board from cupping, rip it in half and glue it back together after first flipping one piece over.

Although it's not necessary to apply glue to both mating edges, I always do, just to make sure both edges are thoroughly wetted.

Clamp the boards together—but don't use excessive pressure, because you might starve the joint. There will be plenty of glue squeezed out, however. I don't recommend wiping it off with a damp cloth, because water seeping into the joint may weaken it. I remove the excess glue with a paint scraper after the glue has set an hour or so (when it's safe to remove the clamps) but before it dries solid. If you let it dry too long, you run the risk of scraping away chunks of wood along with the glue.

If the joint was made and glued properly, it will be stronger than the surrounding wood, and no reinforcement will be necessary. For longer joints, however, the use of a few biscuits or dowels will aid in aligning the faces.

# ▪ Chapter 3 ▪

# DRAWERS, DOORS, AND SHELVES

There are as many ways to make drawers and doors as there are to make cabinets. The kinds of doors and drawers you make, and how you dress them, will depend on the overall style of your entertainment center. What follows is a general discussion on drawers and doors. More details are given in Part II.

## DRAWERS

A drawer is a box. The simplest way to make the box is just to cut five pieces of wood and nail them together. However, drawer construction can be an art in itself. More aesthetically pleasing than nails, for example, is a drawer joined with hand-cut, or machine-cut, dovetails. How you would make a drawer depends not only on what tools you have, but also on how much effort you want to put into it. Certainly, you could spend as much time on a few drawers as you would on the cabinet they fit into.

### Integral Front and Applied Front

Aside from the specific joinery method, there are two broad categories of drawers: integral front and applied front. In the integral-front drawer, shown in Figure 3.1, the front member of the box is made of the same material as the cabinet. Figure 3.2 shows an applied-front drawer. The drawer proper is a box made of 1/2-inch stock, which can be made of any suitable material. A separate front is made of the same material as the rest of the cabinet—typically 3/4 inch thick.

To apply the front, first bore two 1/4-inch-diameter holes through the front of the drawer box. After checking the fit of the drawer in the cabinet and marking the location of the drawer front relative to the drawer, place the front as closely as possible to its final position. Drive two 1 1/8-inch low-profile screws through the inside of the drawer into the applied front. The 1/4-inch holes allow for minor adjustment to the drawer front.

How the drawer front relates to the face of the cabinet is also a consideration. Figure 3.3A shows a flush, or inset, integral-front drawer. Figure 3.3B shows an integral front with a partial, or lipped, overlay—part of the drawer extends beyond the face of the cabinet. Figures 3.3C and D show two variations of full overlay applied-front drawers. C shows a drawer front with a simple ogee (S-shaped) pattern. D is an example of a beveled overlay. This style, popular in the early 1970s, leaves a recessed finger hold, which eliminates the need for knobs or pulls.

Notice that integral-front drawers leave little or no room for adjustment. The beauty of applied-front drawers is that the fronts can move independently of the drawer proper to ensure a good fit.

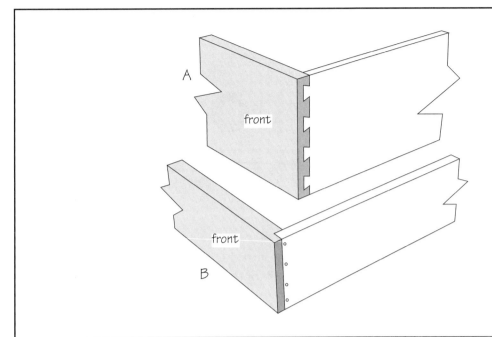

Figure 3.1. Integral fronts: (A) The dovetail joint is interlocking and requires no fasteners other than glue. (B) In the rabbet joint, nails are driven through the drawer sides into the front.

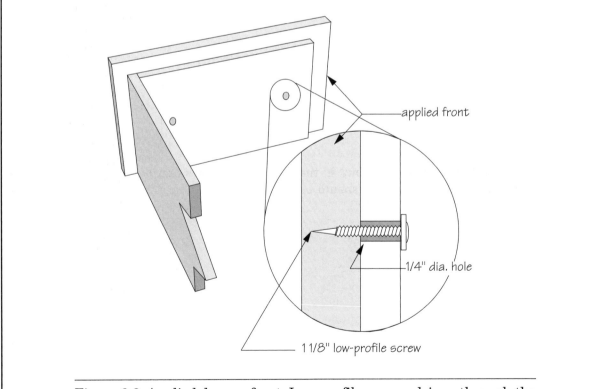

Figure 3.2. Applied drawer front. Low-profile screws driven through the drawer into the front allow for making minor adjustments in alignment.

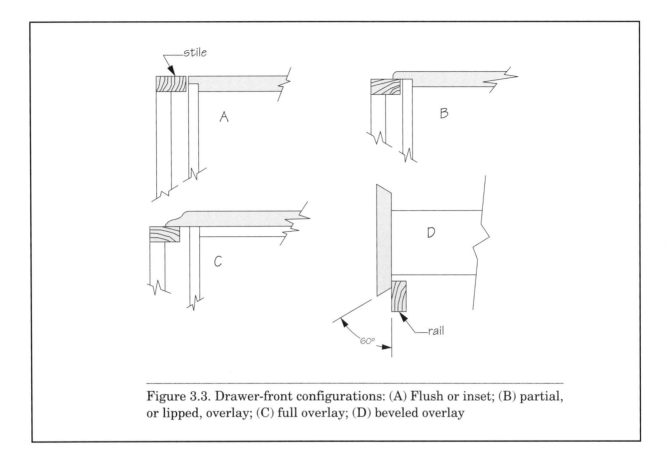

Figure 3.3. Drawer-front configurations: (A) Flush or inset; (B) partial, or lipped, overlay; (C) full overlay; (D) beveled overlay

## Sides, Back, and Bottom

Sides and backs (and the inner front panels of applied-front drawers) are made of 1/2-inch stock. Furniture-grade pine works well for this. Also look for high-grade plywood.

Drawer bottoms are cut from 1/4-inch plywood or other sheet product. The bottoms fit into 1/4-by-1/4-inch grooves cut into the pieces. The groove should be at least 1/4 inch from the bottom of the side, but if the drawer is dovetailed the groove should be fully within the lowermost dovetail.

Figure 3.4A shows how the front, back, and sides are fitted around the bottom. The back is the same width as the sides. Assemble one side to the front and back. Slip the bottom in place and attach the remaining side.

Figure 3.4B shows an alternate way of assembling the back. Cut a dado in each side about 1/2 inch in from the end. The sides are first attached to the front. The back, which is cut to a width equal to the distance from the top of the side to the top edge of the groove for the bottom, is fitted into the dadoes, glued, and nailed. The bottom is then slipped into place under the back. Drive a few brads through the bottom into the back to hold the bottom in place.

## Hardware

Drawer hardware includes knobs, pulls, and slides. Knobs and pulls need little discussion. What kind you choose is a matter of personal choice and cabinet style. Look for good-quality knobs and pulls for extended service and aesthetic value.

What kind of slides you use, however, will make a difference. A drawer that works smoothly is a testimony to quality. The Accuride Series 3832A slide (Figure 3.5) is rated at 100 pounds and is fully extendable—an excellent feature in an entertainment center because it allows easy access to things stored at the back of

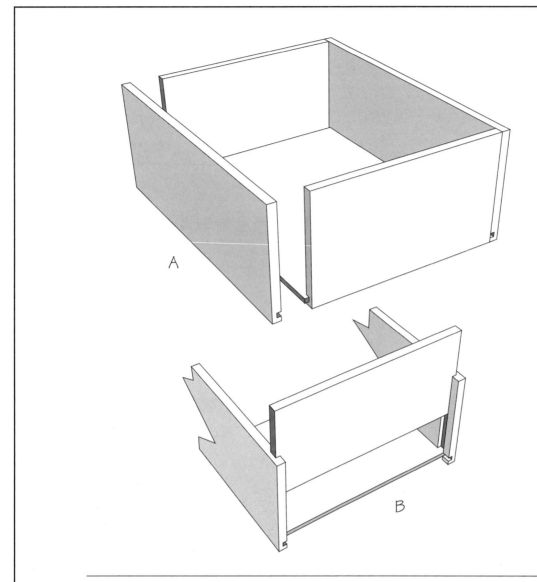

Figure 3.4. Two ways to attach a drawer back. In A, the sides are joined to the front and back in the same manner. The pieces are assembled around the bottom. In B, the sides are first joined to the front in the desired manner. The back slips into dadoes cut into each. The back's width is reduced by the thickness of the drawer bottom and its offset from the bottom edge of the sides. Once the back is fixed to the sides, the bottom is slid into place and tacked to the bottom edge of the back.

the drawer. Where full extension and heavy loads are not factors, consider using lighter, two-thirds-extension slides. Accuride also manufactures full-extension shelf slides (Series 3864).

## DOORS

On your entertainment center, doors can serve one or all of three functions. They can help keep dust away from equipment, hide equipment and stored items, and add to the visual aspects of the cabinet. Like drawers, doors can be simple or complex in construction. Also, they can be flush, full overlay, or partial overlay. A flush door is inset in the cabinet frame. The face of the door is on the same plane as the face of the cabinet. An overlay door sits in front of the face of the cabinet and extends beyond the perimeter of the opening. A partial overlay is lipped, with part of the door inside the opening and part of it extending beyond the opening.

## Flat

The plainest of doors is that cut from a sheet of 3/4-inch plywood. Whether flush or overlay, it can be edge banded or similarly trimmed. A shallow pattern can be routed into the face of the door, or some kind of molding can be applied to add visual interest.

## Frame-and-Panel

Simple panel doors, as shown in Figure 3.6, are easily constructed out of frames of 3/4-inch solid stock and 1/4-inch plywood for the panels. These are visually more interesting than plain doors, and the rails and stiles can be dressed in a pattern to match the rest of the cabinet. Frame stock should be a minimum of 2 inches wide for adequate joint strength.

The stiles have 1/4-inch (minimum) stub tenons in each end, and both rails and stiles have grooves to receive the panel. When cutting the rails to length, don't forget to add the length of the tenons.

Cuts for these doors are easily made on a table saw or table-mounted router. Gluing the panel into place will give added strength to the tenon joints.

Figure 3.5. Accuride slide

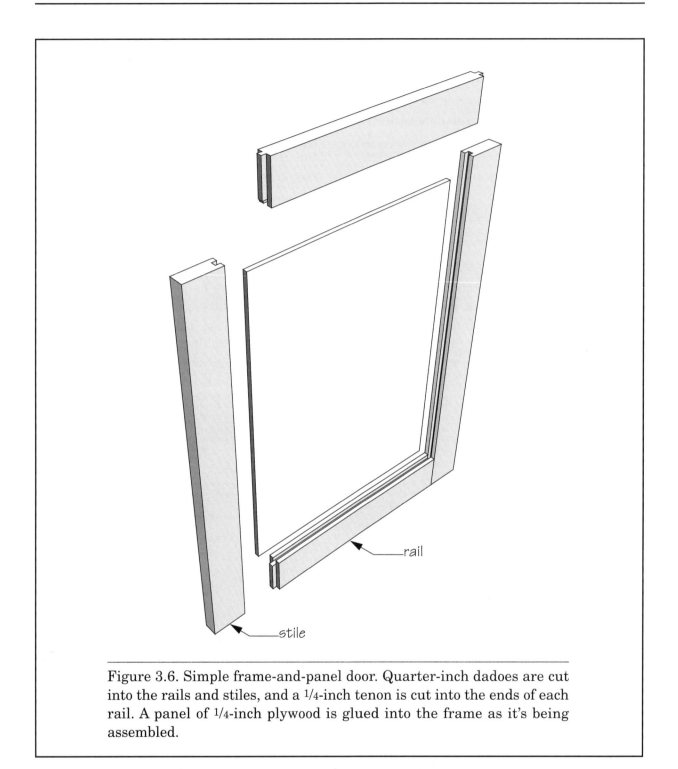

rail

stile

Figure 3.6. Simple frame-and-panel door. Quarter-inch dadoes are cut into the rails and stiles, and a 1/4-inch tenon is cut into the ends of each rail. A panel of 1/4-inch plywood is glued into the frame as it's being assembled.

Raised-panel doors with coped rails and stiles are more complicated to make because they require a shaper or router with a 1/2-inch arbor and special cutting bits. Panels are shaped from solid stock milled to 5/8 inch thick.

## Glass and Grillwork

Doors need not have wood panels. When designing your entertainment center, consider using smoked glass or leaded glass of at least double strength within a wood

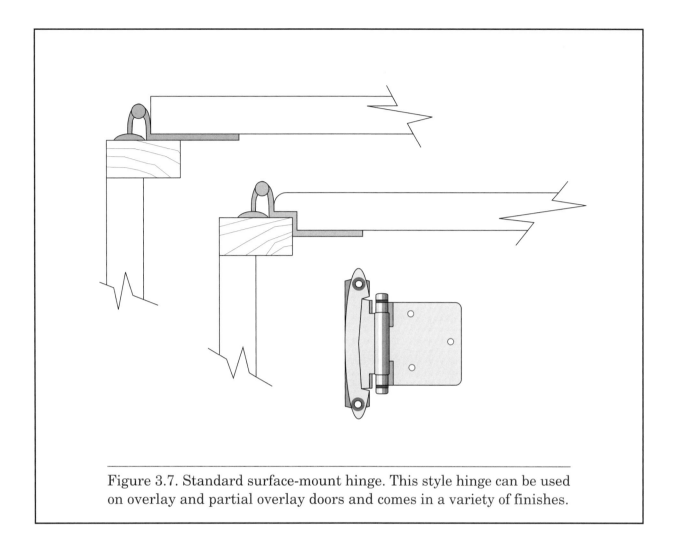

Figure 3.7. Standard surface-mount hinge. This style hinge can be used on overlay and partial overlay doors and comes in a variety of finishes.

frame. If safety is a concern, tempered glass or Plexiglas (plastic) are good choices. In addition, there are a variety of grilles and mesh materials available to use with or without glass.

For glass or grillwork, rabbet your door frames on the backside instead of grooving them. The rabbet should be at least 1/4 inch wide and deep enough to accommodate the panels. Use one of several commercially available retaining clips to hold the panels in place, or make your own.

For glass doors without frames, use plate glass. This requires specialty hinges, pulls, and catches readily available through woodworking catalogs.

## Hinges

Door hinges come in many types, styles, and degrees of quality. What kind of doors you make and the overall style of your entertainment center will determine what kind of hinges you can use. Figure 3.7 shows a typical surface-mount hinge for use on overlay and partial-overlay doors. This kind of hinge comes in several finishes; many are spring-loaded to keep the door closed. Inset doors are hung on butt, strap, butterfly, or T-hinges.

Euro-style hinges (Figure 3.8) are used on overlay doors and are fully concealed when the door is closed. Also, they are recessed into the door—the pivot point is within the recess. Installation of this kind of hinge requires a 1 3/8-inch bit, or a bit of a

Figure 3.8. Concealed Euro-style hinge

diameter as specified by the hinge manufacturer. You must use a drill press or drilling jig to use this bit.

**Flipper Doors.** Flipper doors, also called pocket doors, are designed to conceal the television when it's not in use but to slide out of viewing range when it is. The doors swing on special slides and hinges, as shown in Figure 3.9.

Flipper doors require 2 inches of clearance on each side of the television, limiting the size of the TV that will fit in the opening. If you choose to leave out the doors, the cabinet will accommodate a larger TV.

## ADJUSTABLE SHELVING

There are two reliable methods for installing adjustable shelving. Figure 3.10 shows shelf standards with clips. This method is easy to install and presents a wide range of shelf positions. Shelf standards come in several finishes and can be installed into dadoes routed into the cabinet sides or applied directly to the sides (with the shelves cut shorter to compensate). They can be cut to length and need not run the full height of the cabinet.

Pins, shown in Figure 3.11, are set in holes bored directly into the cabinet sides at regular intervals—the smaller the interval, the more shelf positions you have. Pins are less expensive and less conspicuous than standards. They come in steel, brass, and plastic. You can also make your own out of wooden dowel stock. Purchase all the pins you need before drilling any holes to be sure you have a bit that exactly matches the pin diameter. Use a drill or plunge router to make the holes. Be careful: lack of precision here will mean wobbly or lopsided shelves. You can also make or purchase a jig to keep the holes in perfect alignment.

Figure 3.9. Flipper-door hinge mechanism

Figure 3.10. Shelf standards can be recessed into dadoes cut into the cabinet sides, as shown, or mounted to the surface.

Figure 3.11. Careful layout of pin-holes is essential.

# • Chapter 4 •

# FINISHING NOTES

A good finish serves several purposes. It seals the wood, thereby lessening the effects of changes in humidity; it protects the wood against damage from day-to-day use; and it enhances the wood's natural beauty.

Finishing is as much a craft as woodworking. Achieving professional results in finishing takes practice. Without proper preparation and without the use of the best tools and materials available, the results will be less than satisfying.

Some professionals and experienced woodworkers stick to their own formulas and methods. Others tend to experiment to achieve a specific result. Fortunately, many products on the market today have been developed for ease of application by the do-it-yourselfer.

Several manufacturers offer systems of compatible products. If you're inexperienced at finishing, look into one of these systems.

## SANDING

The first step to a good finish is to sand the piece thoroughly to prepare the wood for the finish. This is done in stages, beginning with a course sandpaper and progressing to finer and finer grits. Grit refers to the number of abrasive particles per square inch of paper. The lower the number, the coarser the paper; 80-grit is coarser than 100-grit.

What grit to begin with and how many stages to go through depend on the wood and its condition. In most cases, either 100-grit or 150-grit is a good choice to start with. But if you start with a paper coarser than necessary, you'll be doing a lot of extra work. The same is true if you start with too fine a grit. More than once I've had to drop down to a coarser grit after getting nowhere with my first choice.

A good progression to follow is 100, 150, 180, 220. This recommendation is for finish sanding only. It's likely that you'll need a coarser grit during assembly—for example, to even out a glue joint or to knock down some saw marks.

## STAINING

Applying a stain to a piece of furniture is not necessary unless you want to enhance the wood or attempt to match existing furniture. Many woods have variations in their grain pattern due to the difference in hardness between springwood and summerwood: wood is softer and lighter if it forms relatively early in the growing season. Staining the wood will make these variations all the more striking. This may or may not be desirable. Always test the stain on a few pieces of scrap from different boards. To obtain a more uniform color, apply a coat of penetrating clear sealer before staining. Be aware that a water-soluble stain will raise the grain, requiring yet another thorough resanding.

## FILLING AND SEALING

Hardwoods with large pores—oak, walnut, and mahogany, for example—should be filled before you add the top coat. Fillers come in liquid and paste form. Fillers are brushed or rubbed onto the wood, with and across the grain, and then the excess is wiped off before it has time to dry.

Applying a sealer is the last step before applying the top coats. Sealers prevent absorption of the top coats. They dry fast and are easy to sand, producing a smooth, clean substrate for the top coats.

### Solvents and Hazards

Conventional finishing materials have as their vehicle solvents and other ingredients that release volatile organic compounds (VOCs) into the air as they dry. These VOCs have been found to be harmful to the atmosphere—not to mention the people who use them. Manufacturers have responded by developing water-soluble finishing products that are considered environmentally safe.

Environmental concerns aside, water-soluble materials offer other benefits. They are nonflammable and release no explosive fumes. There is no need for flammable solvents for thinning and cleanup, as thinning is usually unnecessary and cleanup is with soap and water. In addition, these products dry faster, so projects are completed sooner.

Any finish needs to be sanded between coats. Many finishers use 0000 steel wool for this purpose. Do not use steel wool on water-soluble stains and finishes. Tiny particles of steel left in the pores will rust. Wet-or-dry paper (400–600) is best for this.

## TOP COATING

Traditional top coats include varnish, shellac, lacquer, and wax. Each of these requires a certain amount of sanding and buffing between coats to provide the desired effect.

An excellent coating for the do-it-yourselfer is one of the many polyurethane products. They are relatively easy to apply, and two or three coats are sufficient for a tough, durable surface.

An oil finish, such as Watco Oil, is also a popular choice. It's the easiest to apply. Two coats are brushed on liberally, and then allowed to sit for maximum absorption before the excess is wiped off. Once dry (two to three days), a paste wax can be applied, but it's not necessary. With an oil finish, you don't need to stain the wood beforehand. When the finish gets dull, you can revive it with another application. However, an oil finish doesn't offer the same qualities of protection and luster as a true top coat.

# Part II: The Cabinets

## ▪ Chapter 5 ▪

# PLANNING YOUR ENTERTAINMENT CENTER

The primary function of any entertainment center is to hold audiovisual equipment and media. You'll want to make sure the center you build will accommodate what you have and what you're likely to acquire.

Of course, the first thing you'll want to accommodate is the television, which will take up more space than any other single electronic component. Everything else is built around the television unit. This being the case, it's important to know the dimensions of your television before beginning.

The table below gives the dimensions of several televisions (screen sizes measured diagonally), as well as other useful dimensions. Whereas the dimensions of videocassettes and compact disk "jewel cases" (the plastic boxes individual CDs come in) are constant, those of audio-visual components are not. The ranges given in the table are based on random samplings of dozens of components.

Before beginning, give careful thought to the style you wish to achieve. You'll notice that all the plans depict cabinets of a plain, unadorned style. In chapter 9, I offer several ways to customize the generic designs to suit a variety of tastes. Take special note of the discussion "Trimming the Bottom and Top."

What kind of wood you use will convey a certain style by itself. For example, pine suggests a simple Colonial or early American style. For a richer traditional look, cherry and walnut are good choices. Mahogany also has a rich appearance. Oak has a contemporary feel.

## Dimensions (in inches)

| Item | Width | Height | Depth |
|------|-------|--------|-------|
| VHS cassette | $7^3/_8$ | $4^1/_{16}$ | 1 |
| CD "jewel case" | $4^{15}/_{16}$ | $5^5/_8$ | $7/_{16}$ |
| 19" TV | 19–20 | 18–20 | 20 |
| 27" TV | $24^1/_4$–$26^1/_2$ | 22–24 | 20 |
| 32" TV | $30^1/_2$–$31^1/_2$ | 25–$26^1/_2$ | 24 |
| 35" TV | $34^1/_4$–$35^1/_2$ | $31^1/_2$–$32^1/_4$ | 22–25 |
| VCR | $14^1/_2$–15 | $3^1/_2$–4 | 10–13 |
| Audio component | $16^1/_2$–17 | $3^1/_2$–8 | $11^1/_2$–$15^1/_2$ |

Perhaps the biggest factor in the planning of your entertainment center is the size of the room it will be in. The various sizes and possible combinations of the modules give you a lot of latitude.

## CONFIGURATIONS

The basic unit of the entertainment center is the television cabinet. In fact, any one of the television cabinets (or side cabinets, if you don't want to include a television) could stand alone as an entertainment center. But the idea behind the entertainment center is to house all of your audiovisual equipment, so it likely would be necessary to add one, two, or even four side cabinets to the television cabinet. Illustrated here in Figures 5.1 and 5.2 are twenty possible combinations of cabinets composed of the eight television-cabinet designs and four side-cabinet designs. The television cabinets are numbered 6A–6H and the side cabinets 7A–7D. Both sets of cabinets are further identified by their dimensions of width, height, and depth, which, in most cases, are given in whole numbers. Actual fractional dimensions are rounded down for the nominal description. Notice that a given entertainment center can be flush or offset across the front and top.

In chapters 6 and 7 are plans for all twelve cabinets. The television cabinets come in four heights, two widths and two depths. All include a space for a VCR, a cassette drawer, and storage. Some have open spaces for display. The side cabinets come in two heights and two depths. These can be used for audiovisual equipment, storage, or display.

Notice that the television modules are in two depths, 21 inches and 24 inches nominally. Notice also, in the preceding table, that the range of television depths is from about 20 inches for a 19-inch TV to 25 inches for a 35-inch TV. The implication here is that some of the larger televisions may not be fully enclosed front-to-back within a given TV module. Although a deeper cabinet can of course be built, matters of practicality and economy of materials where 4-by-8-foot sheets of plywood are concerned precluded the designing of deeper units. If necessary, the larger televisions can protrude slightly beyond the front or back of the cabinet.

## MATERIALS

Once you've decided what to build, it's time to begin gathering the necessary materials. Most woodworking projects presented in books and magazines are accompanied by a list of materials, which gives materials by rough dimension and quantity, or a cutting list, which gives exact dimensions for each piece. I find a list of materials more helpful, primarily because if I make an adjustment here or there to suit my needs, a cutting list quickly becomes useless.

A list of materials is fine for a single project. But here we have a combination of several. It would be impossible (for me, anyway) to figure out a basic materials list for each combination. Combining lists of materials for individual modules is a start, but it still presents a problem, especially where sheet goods are concerned. Take, for example, a module that requires a little more than one and a half sheets of 3/4-inch plywood. You would likely buy two sheets of plywood, knowing that there will be some waste. But what if you planned to build and combine three similar units? Taken as a whole, you'd need only five sheets, not six.

### Sheet Stock

At first glance it would seem that the easiest way to determine sheet-stock needs is to figure the total square footage necessary and divide by 32 (the number of square feet in a 4-by-8-foot sheet). This method, however, is flawed and could lead to a shortage. For example, your project requires five pieces 12 inches wide and 54 inches long. Each piece is 4 1/2 square feet; all five of them come to 22 1/2 square feet, well within

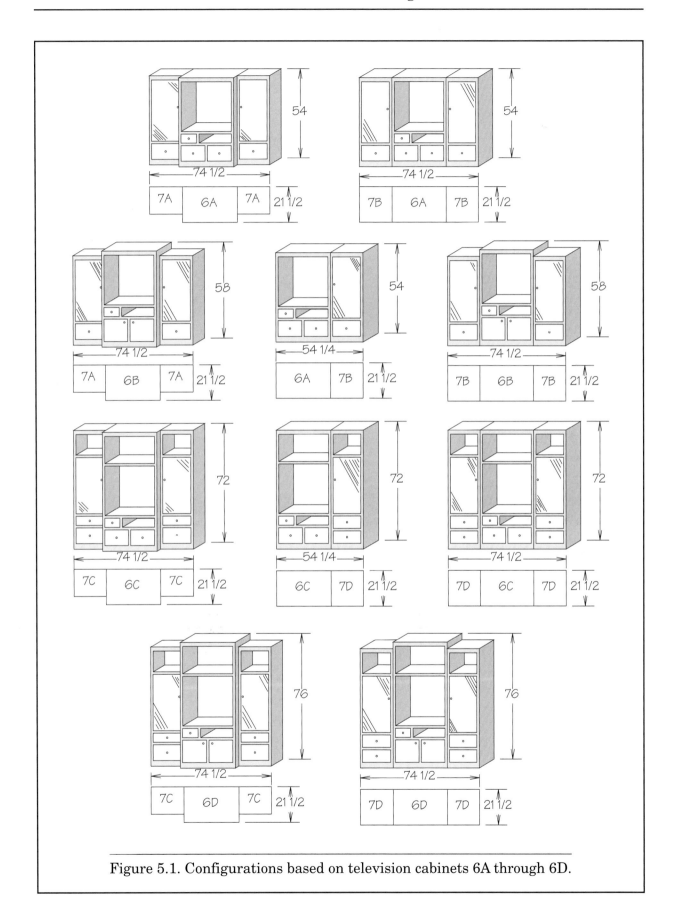

Figure 5.1. Configurations based on television cabinets 6A through 6D.

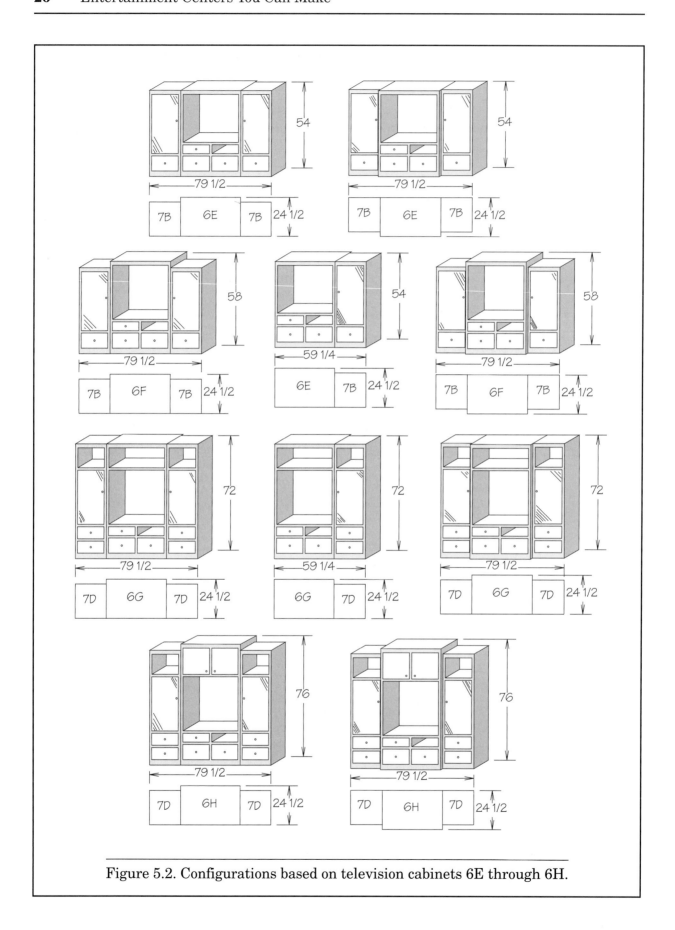

Figure 5.2. Configurations based on television cabinets 6E through 6H.

the 32 square-foot limitation of one sheet. Figure 5.3 shows why you'll need another sheet. Unless you can talk your supplier into chopping up another sheet and selling a portion of it by the square foot, you'll end up needing to buy a second sheet.

With the drawings for each module, you'll find suggested cutting schemes for the major plywood components. By combining schemes from two or three modules, you can more easily visualize how to make the best use out of the fewest sheets. It might be necessary to redraw multiple cutting schemes to arrive at a more efficient use of the plywood. Use graph paper or lay out a rectangle 4 by 8 inches on a piece of blank paper as a template. Don't forget to take saw kerfs into account. You can't rip a sheet of plywood in half and get two pieces exactly 24 inches wide.

Usually you'll cut your plywood pieces so that the grain runs along the length of the piece. That's the advantage to using ply-

wood; you have a large surface to work with. Whereas it might be desirable to have the grain of a given piece run lengthwise, it isn't always necessary. Figure 6D.2 illustrates an example. Notice the cutting scheme at the top of the drawing. Four of the fixed shelves are laid out so their grain runs lengthwise— the preferred direction. The grain of the bottom shelf, however, runs across the length. In order to get a shelf to match the others, you'd need another sheet. The bottom shelf will be concealed within the cabinet, making the direction of the grain irrelevant. To get the most out of your plywood—thus saving on material costs—cut such pieces any way you can.

## Solid Stock

Estimating solid lumber presents similar problems, but with judicious shopping, waste can be kept to a minimum. Remember, however, that when dealing with boards that are

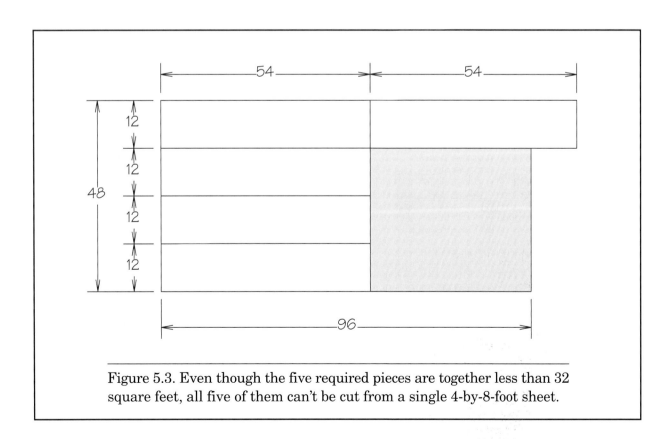

Figure 5.3. Even though the five required pieces are together less than 32 square feet, all five of them can't be cut from a single 4-by-8-foot sheet.

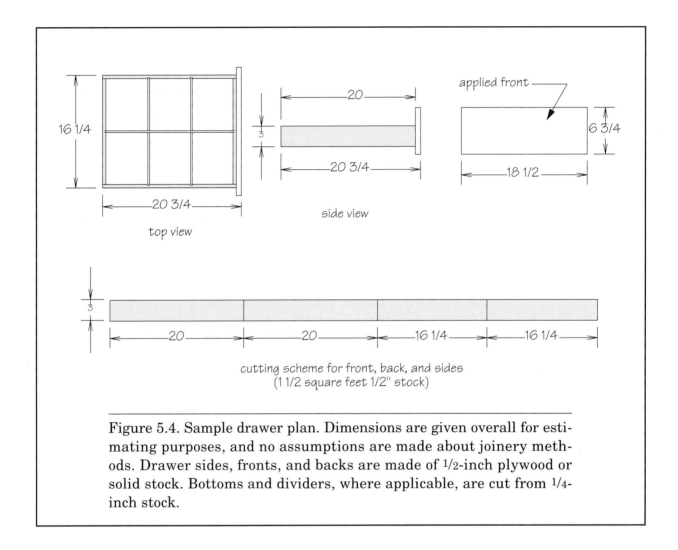

16 1/4

20 3/4

top view

20

3

20 3/4

side view

applied front

6 3/4

18 1/2

3

20

20

16 1/4

16 1/4

cutting scheme for front, back, and sides
(1 1/2 square feet 1/2" stock)

Figure 5.4. Sample drawer plan. Dimensions are given overall for estimating purposes, and no assumptions are made about joinery methods. Drawer sides, fronts, and backs are made of 1/2-inch plywood or solid stock. Bottoms and dividers, where applicable, are cut from 1/4-inch stock.

nominally 1 inch thick (4/4 or 1-by stock) a board foot is the same as a square foot.

Just knowing how many board feet or square feet of lumber you'll need is not enough. Neither is having an exact cutting list. Hardwood lumber is sold in random lengths and widths, and you have to pick from what's available on a given day. The trick is to figure out on the spot how you can get all the pieces you need from a collection of long, short, skinny, and wide boards. The next trick is to remember how you planned to cut up all those boards when you get them back to the shop. There will always be waste, but if you plan right, there won't be as much.

Along with the plywood cutting scheme for each module, you'll find a visual layout of all the major solid pieces. This includes face-frame rails and stiles, aprons, and fronts for applied-front drawers. Drawer fronts are assumed to be applied with a 5/8-inch overlay all the way around, which will yield a 1/4-inch space between adjoining doors and drawers. Included with the layout is an estimate of how many board feet the project will need. This estimate includes 15 to 20 percent for waste.

There also is a cutting scheme for the 1/4-inch components. Use a panel (plywood or otherwise) with the same face veneer as the rest of the cabinet. You can substitute a less expensive product for drawer bottoms. The 1/4-inch cutting scheme also includes dimensions for panels for frame-and-panel doors.

The dimensions given allow for the panel to fit into a 1/4-inch-deep dado cut in the frame stock. If you'd rather make raised-panel doors, the additional solid stock needed is shown on the solid-stock cutting scheme that accompanies each plan.

## Notes on the Plans

Drawer plans accompany the module plans that have a drawer or drawers and include a visual representation of all the pieces for a single drawer of a given dimension. Because exact measurements of the various drawer components depend on the method of joinery, dimensions given in the plans will be overall, as shown in Figure 5.4, with allowances made for 1/2-inch clearance on each side for a typical drawer slide. The slides you use will also have an impact on drawer dimensions. You'll find more discussion of drawers and doors in chapter 9.

Incidental pieces such as trim, molding, edge bands, cleats, spacers, and other blocks can be made from scrap and are not included in any cutting scheme.

Because all of the cabinets can be assembled in the same manner, general assembly instructions are given in chapter 9.

## Hardware Checklist

All of the modules require hardware of one kind or another. I recommend that you purchase the hardware before beginning your entertainment center. This will ensure that you build to the right specifications regarding the hardware and there will be no surprises. If you order your hardware from a catalog, allow at least two weeks for shipping. See the Appendix for a list of hardware suppliers and other items of interest to woodworkers.

Rather than giving a list of hardware for each module, I have instead assembled the following overall checklist of hardware and other materials you'll need.

• Glue. Elmer's Carpenter's glue and Titebond wood glue are standards.

• Brads and finish nails of various sizes for nailing on cabinet backs and moldings.

• Wood screws or drywall screws.

• Drawer slides.

• Hinges and catches.

• Knobs and pulls.

• Shelf pins, or standards and brackets.

• Casters and levelers.

• Fastening devices (for bolting individual units together).

# ▪ Chapter 6 ▪

# TELEVISION CABINETS

The eight television cabinets are numbered 6A through 6H (Figure 6.1). Units 6A through 6D are 34 inches wide and 21 inches deep, and units 6E through 6H are 39 inches wide and 24 inches deep. These two sets of cabinets come in four heights: 54, 58, 72, and 76 inches. The 54- and 72-inch heights correspond with the 54- and 72-inch side cabinets to create a finished entertainment center that is flush along the top. The 58- and 76-inch television cabinets are designed 4 inches taller than their respective side cabinets to create a stepped effect in the fully assembled product.

Each of the 34-inch cabinets has a television recess 31 inches wide and 30 inches tall. This will accommodate most TVs up to 27 inches (screen measured diagonally) and some 32-inch TVs (see table on page 23).

Of the four 39-inch cabinets, 6E has a television cavity 36 inches wide by 30 inches tall, which will hold most 32-inch televisions. The other three have 36-inch by 34-inch cavities, large enough for a 35-inch TV.

All of the drawings for the television cabinets call for backs made of 1/4-inch sheet stock with the same surface wood as that of the face frame. The back has a cutout that gives easy access for running cords and cables. The cutout also will allow the rearmost portion of the deeper television models to protrude beyond the rear of the cabinet, thus making room for flipper doors on the front of the cabinet, if you want them and if you have enough space. Remember that flipper doors will require 2 inches on each side of the television. The dimensions given for the cutouts are arbitrary, however; depending on the actual size of the television, it may be necessary to adjust the dimensions to ensure adequate clearance and accessibility while at the same time concealing the wall behind the cabinet.

The cabinet plans are not absolute. Chapter 9, "Variations, Options, and Ideas," offers ways in which you can modify the plans to get more out of your entertainment center.

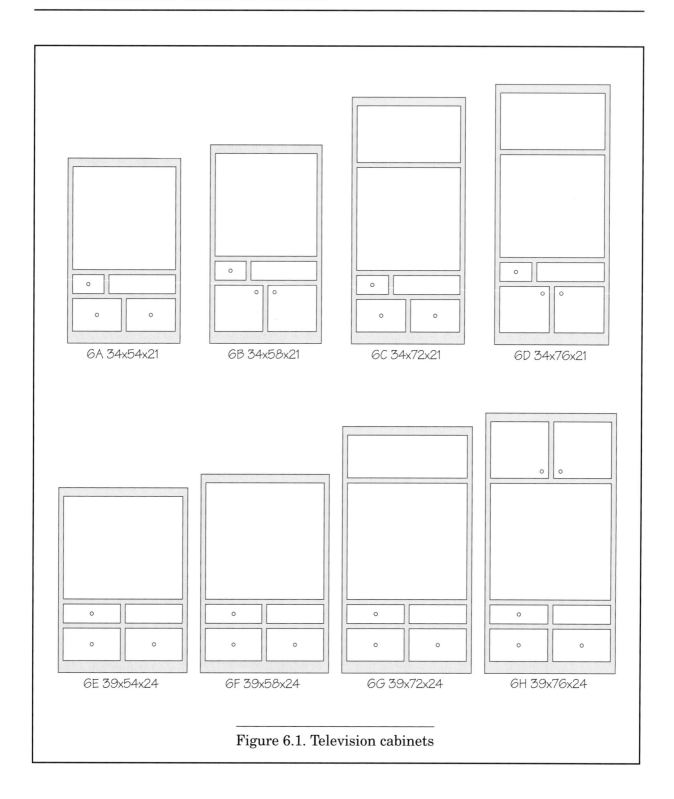

6A 34x54x21        6B 34x58x21        6C 34x72x21        6D 34x76x21

6E 39x54x24        6F 39x58x24        6G 39x72x24        6H 39x76x24

Figure 6.1. Television cabinets

## CABINET 6A: 34 X 54 X 21

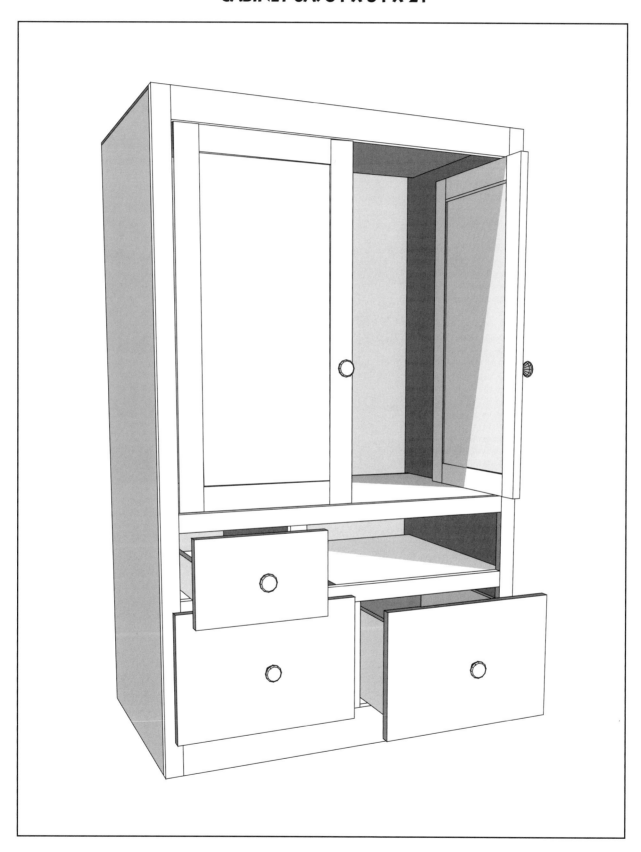

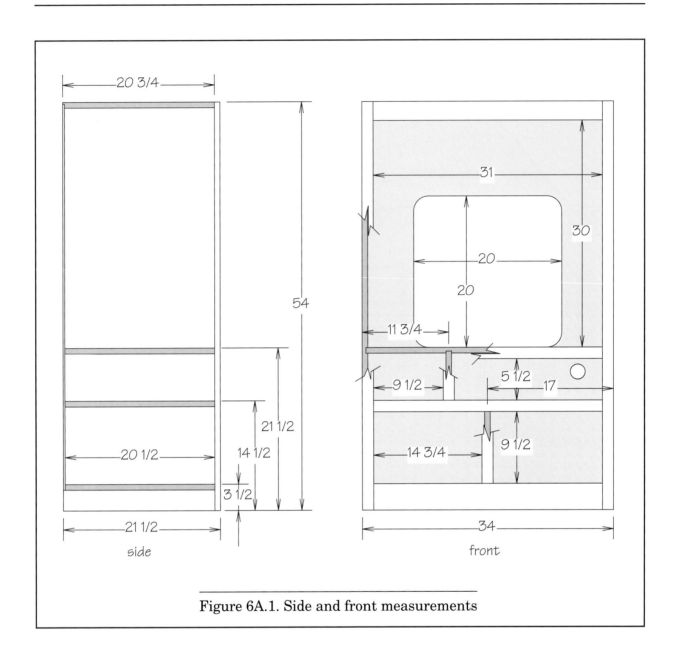

Figure 6A.1. Side and front measurements

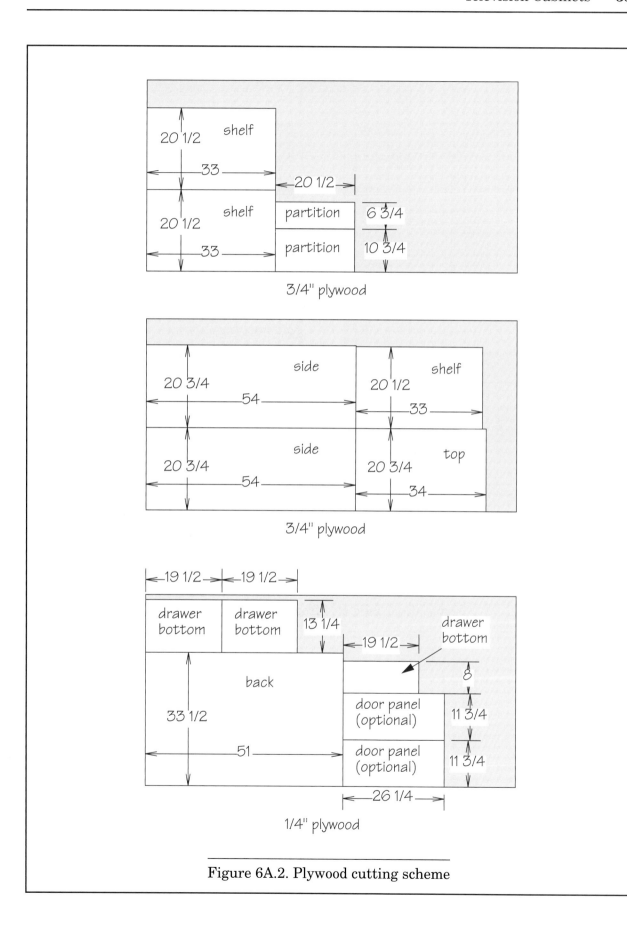

Figure 6A.2. Plywood cutting scheme

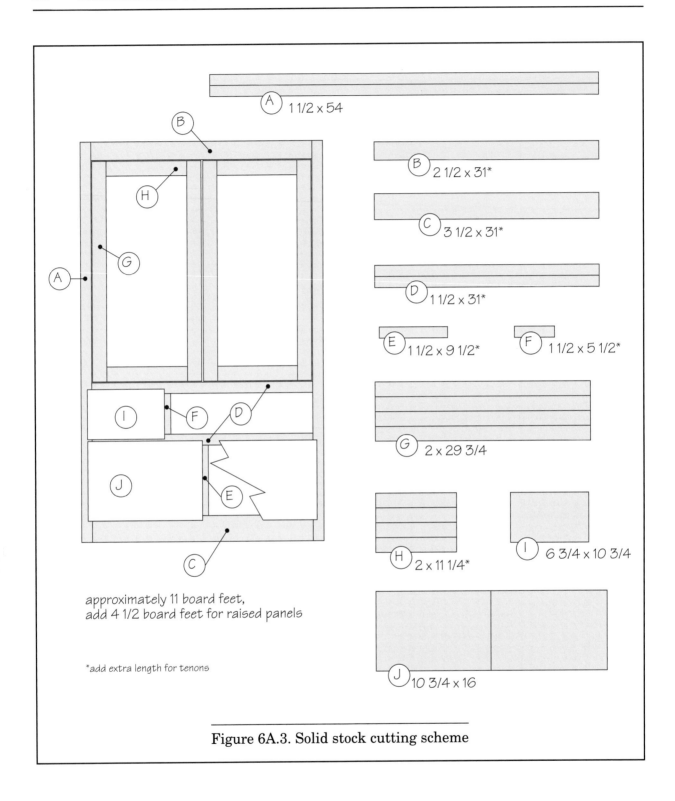

A 1 1/2 x 54

B 2 1/2 x 31*

C 3 1/2 x 31*

D 1 1/2 x 31*

E 1 1/2 x 9 1/2*

F 1 1/2 x 5 1/2*

G 2 x 29 3/4

H 2 x 11 1/4*

I 6 3/4 x 10 3/4

J 10 3/4 x 16

approximately 11 board feet,
add 4 1/2 board feet for raised panels

*add extra length for tenons

Figure 6A.3. Solid stock cutting scheme

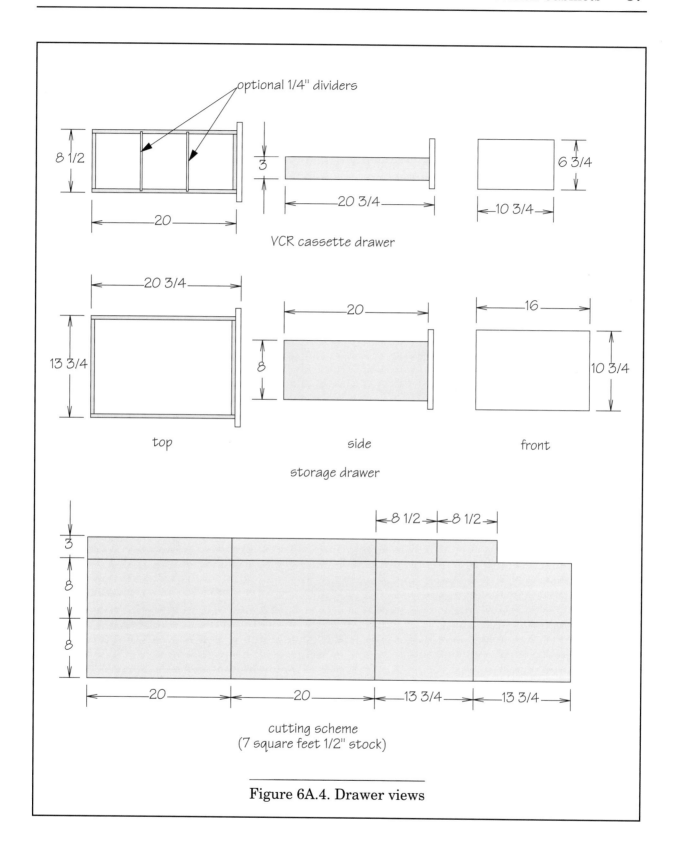

optional 1/4" dividers

8 1/2

20

3

20 3/4

6 3/4

10 3/4

VCR cassette drawer

20 3/4

13 3/4

20

8

16

10 3/4

top

side

front

storage drawer

8 1/2    8 1/2

3

8

8

20    20    13 3/4    13 3/4

cutting scheme
(7 square feet 1/2" stock)

Figure 6A.4. Drawer views

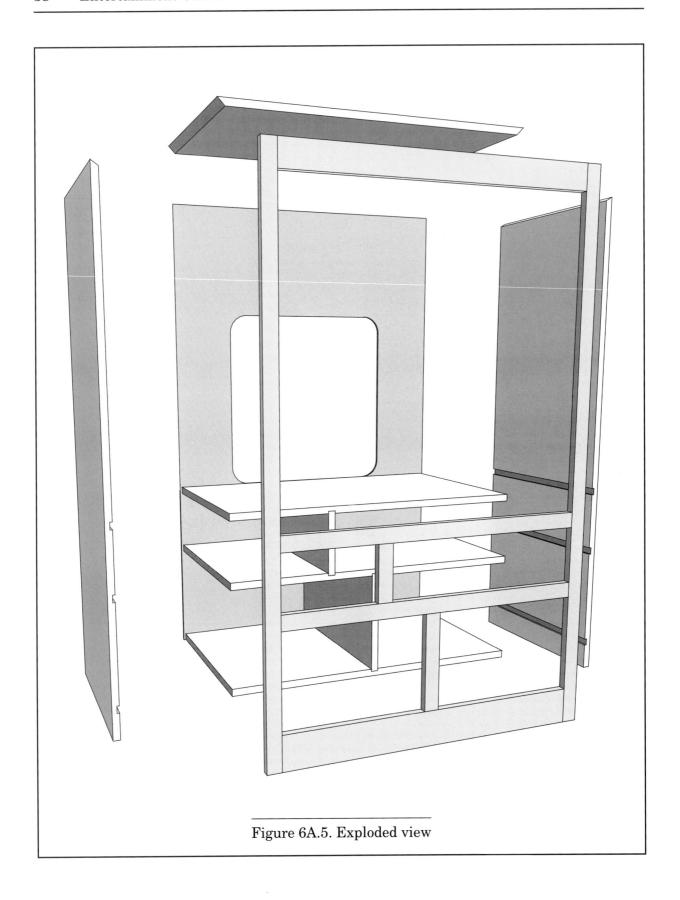

Figure 6A.5. Exploded view

## CABINET 6B: 34 X 58 X 21

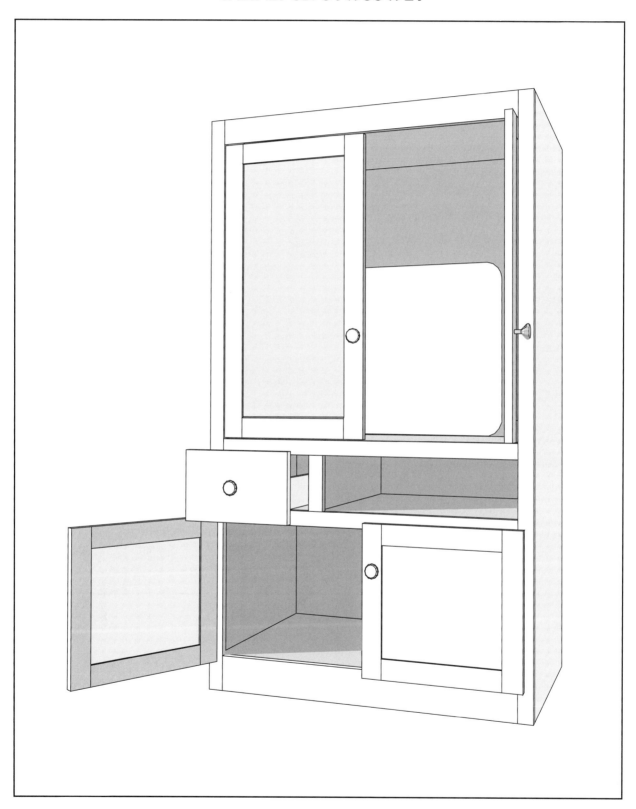

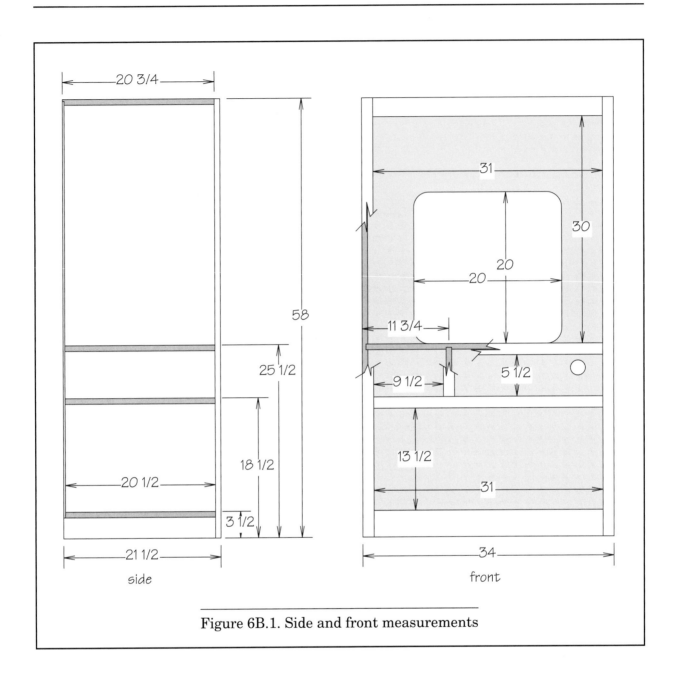

Figure 6B.1. Side and front measurements

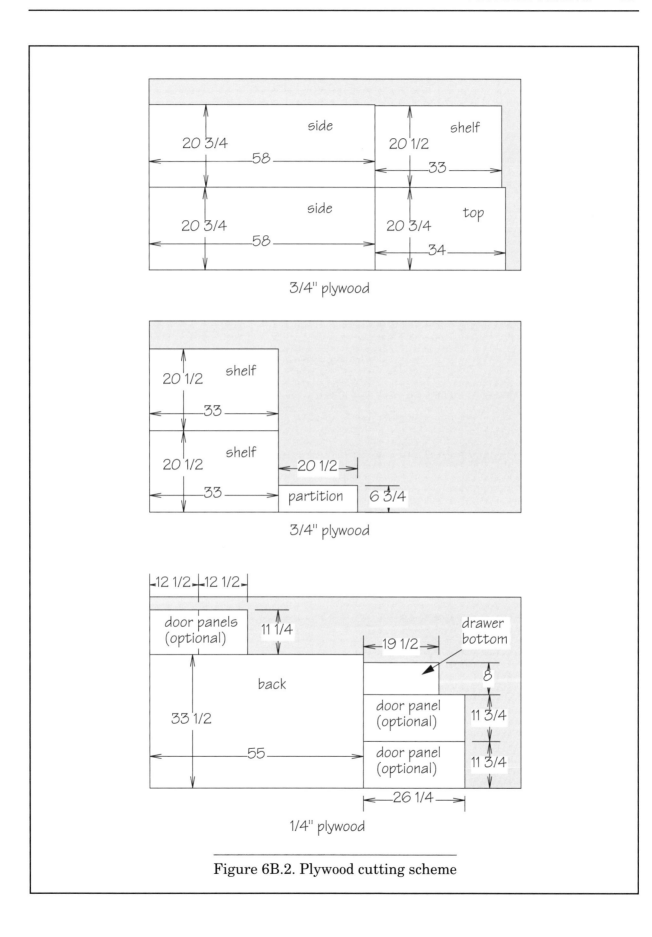

Figure 6B.2. Plywood cutting scheme

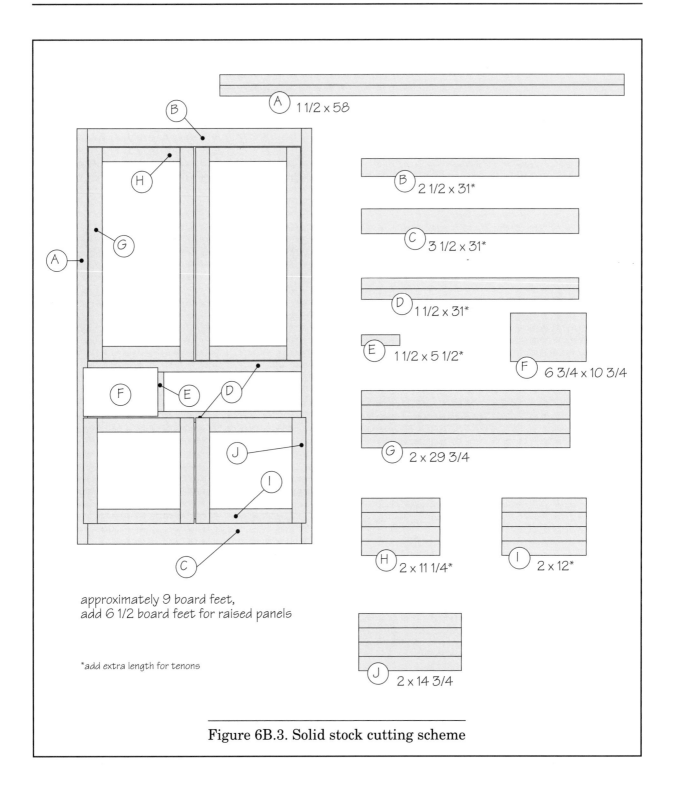

approximately 9 board feet,
add 6 1/2 board feet for raised panels

*add extra length for tenons

Figure 6B.3. Solid stock cutting scheme

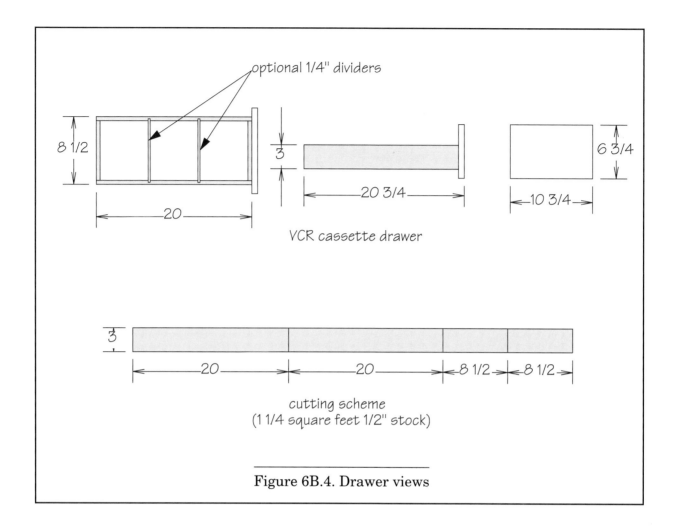

optional 1/4" dividers

8 1/2

20

3

20 3/4

VCR cassette drawer

6 3/4

10 3/4

3

20

20

8 1/2

8 1/2

cutting scheme
(1 1/4 square feet 1/2" stock)

Figure 6B.4. Drawer views

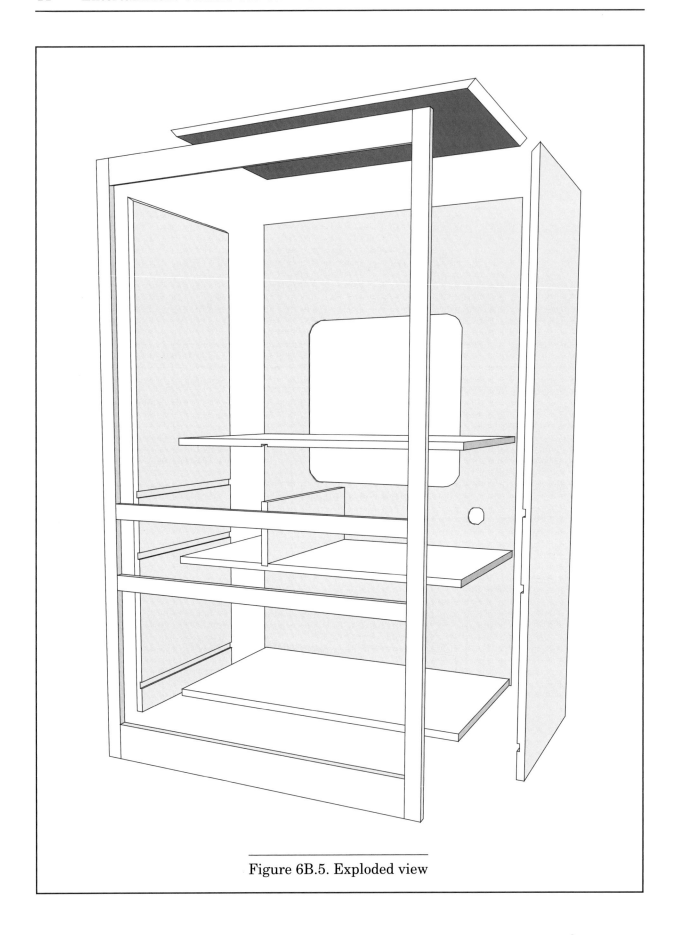

Figure 6B.5. Exploded view

## CABINET 6C: 34 X 72 X 21

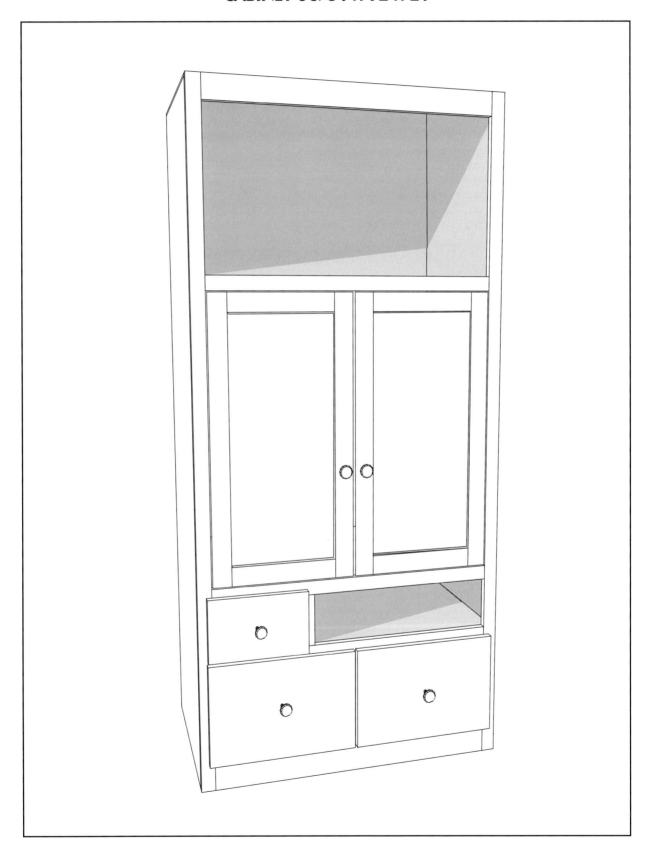

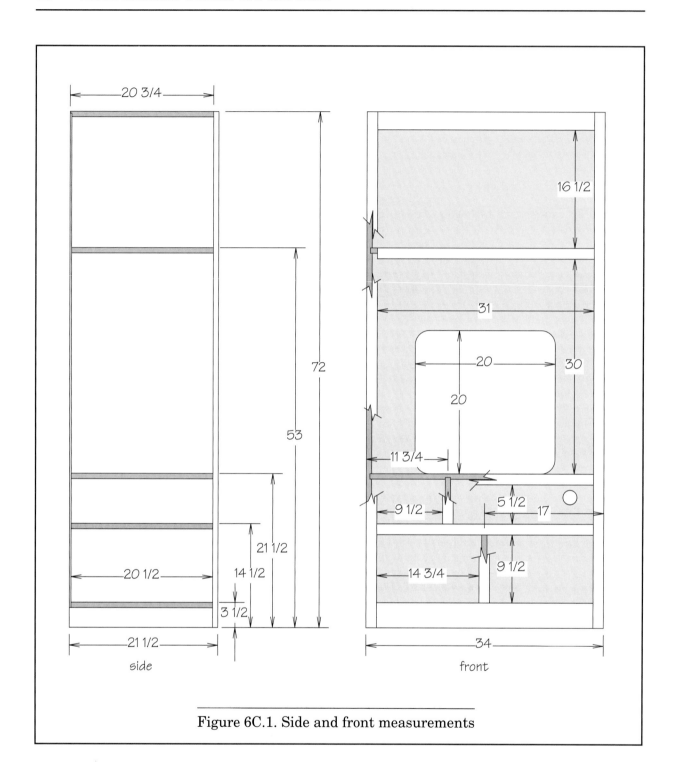

Figure 6C.1. Side and front measurements

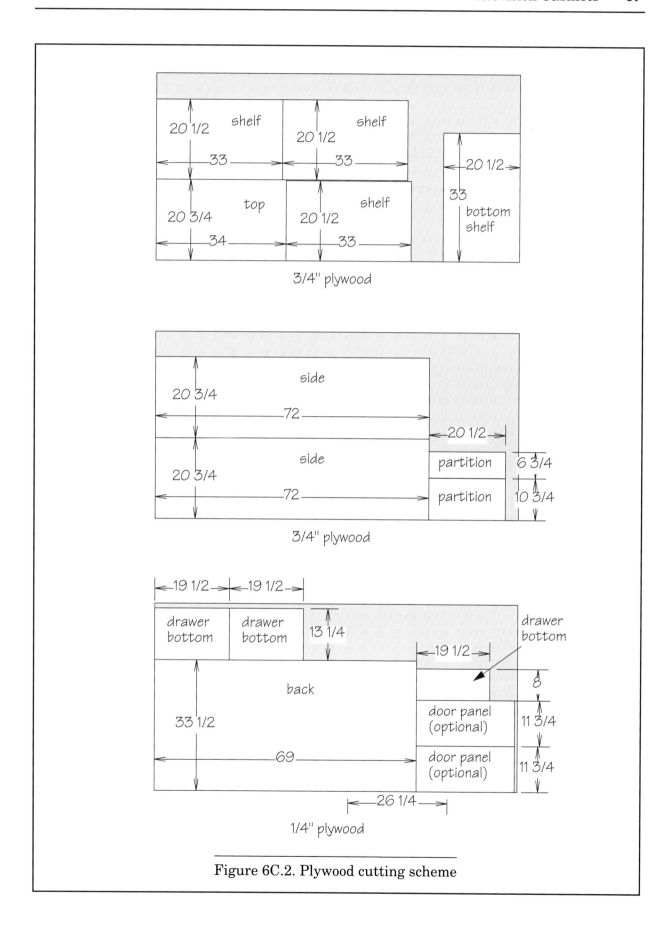

Figure 6C.2. Plywood cutting scheme

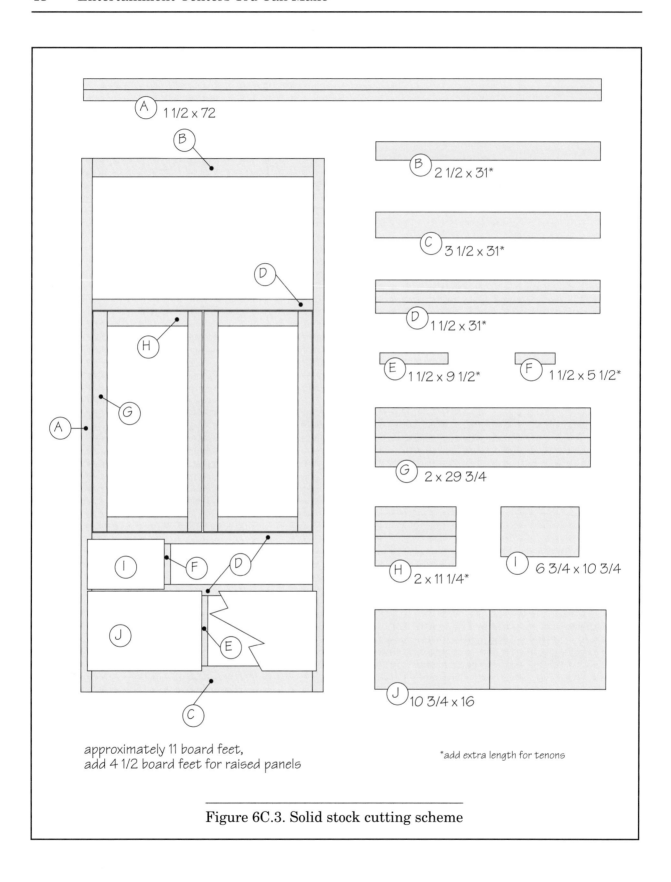

A 1 1/2 x 72

B 2 1/2 x 31*

C 3 1/2 x 31*

D 1 1/2 x 31*

E 1 1/2 x 9 1/2*

F 1 1/2 x 5 1/2*

G 2 x 29 3/4

H 2 x 11 1/4*

I 6 3/4 x 10 3/4

J 10 3/4 x 16

approximately 11 board feet,
add 4 1/2 board feet for raised panels

*add extra length for tenons

Figure 6C.3. Solid stock cutting scheme

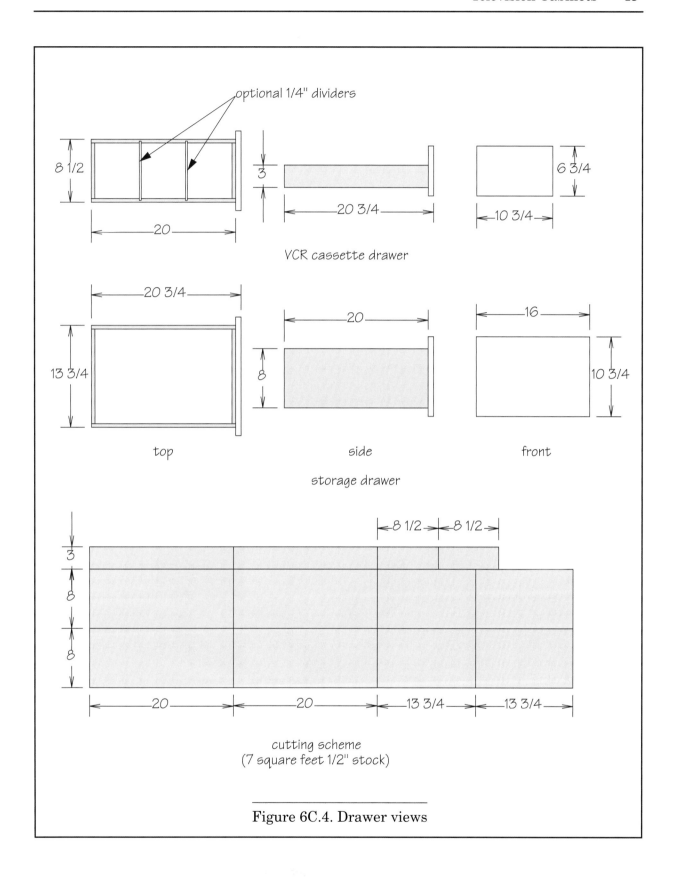

Figure 6C.4. Drawer views

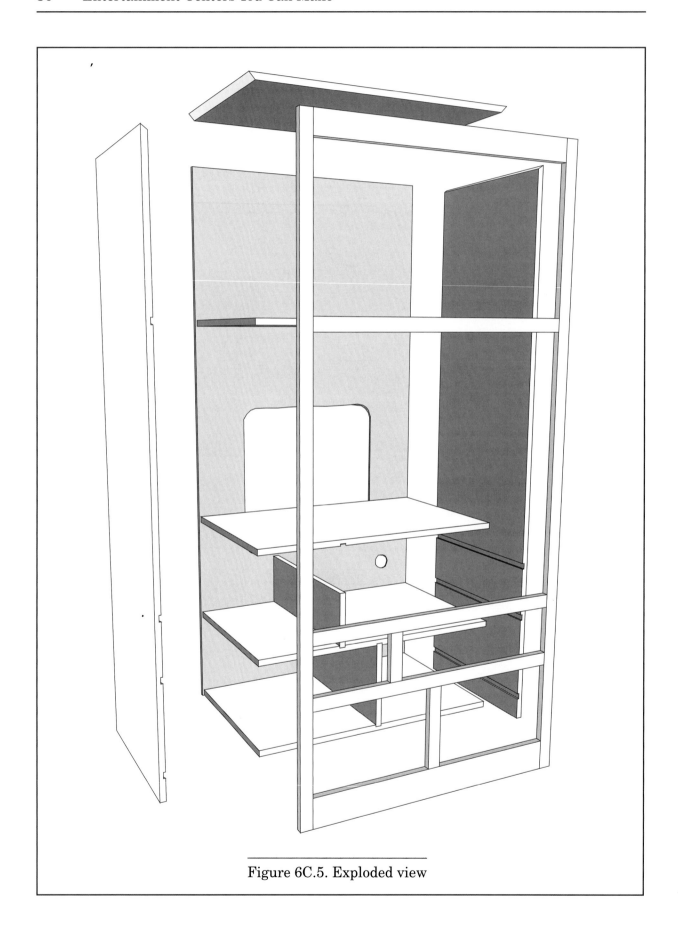

Figure 6C.5. Exploded view

## CABINET 6D: 34 X 76 X 21

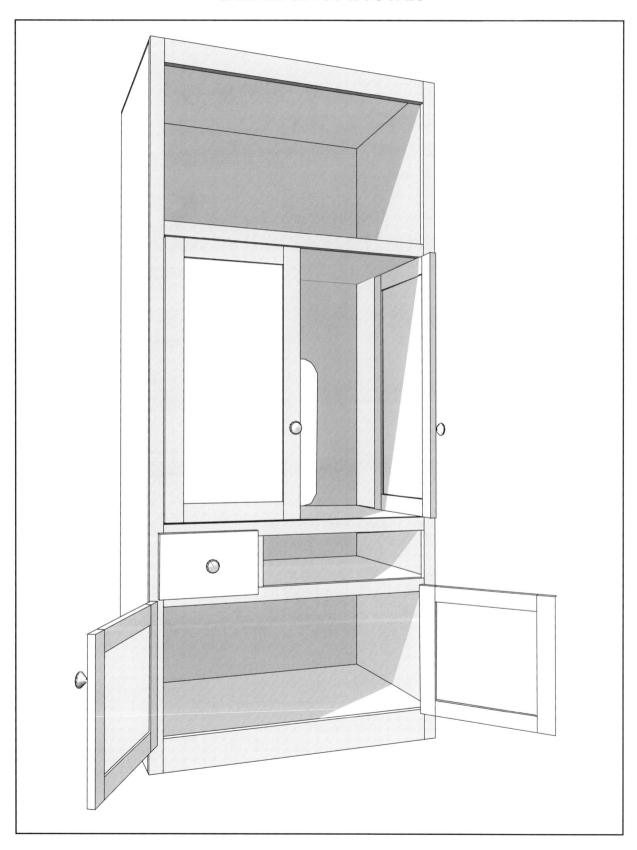

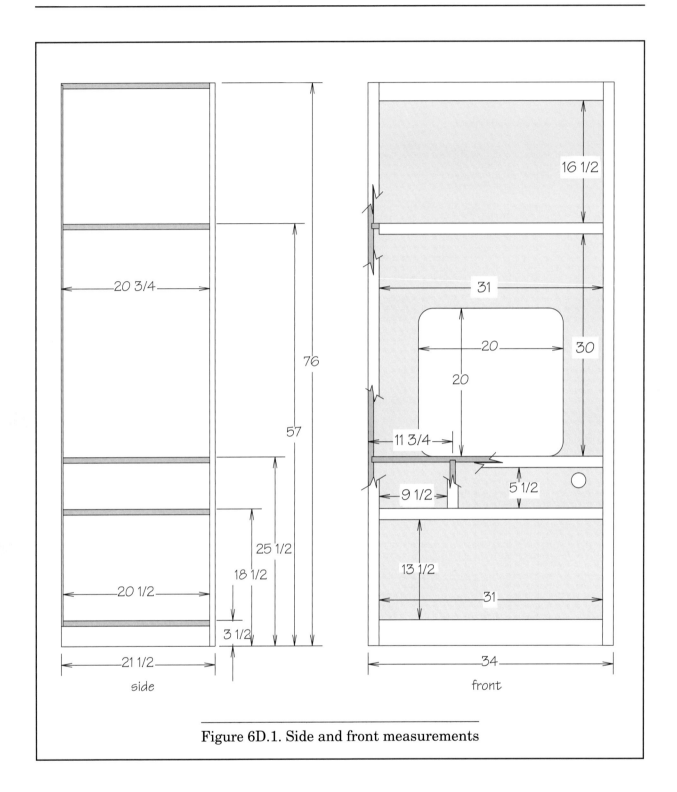

Figure 6D.1. Side and front measurements

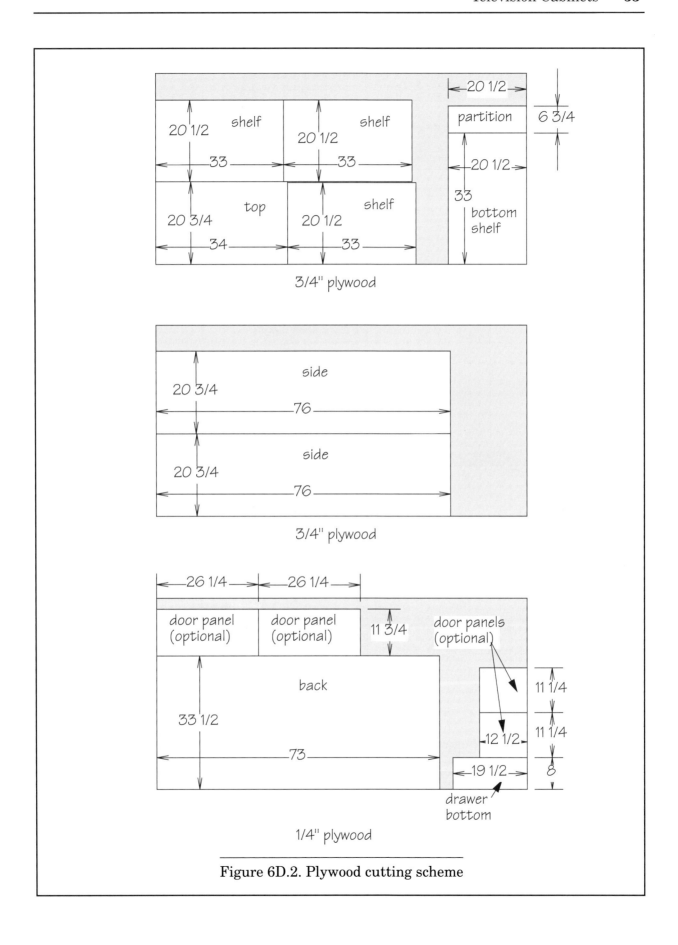

Figure 6D.2. Plywood cutting scheme

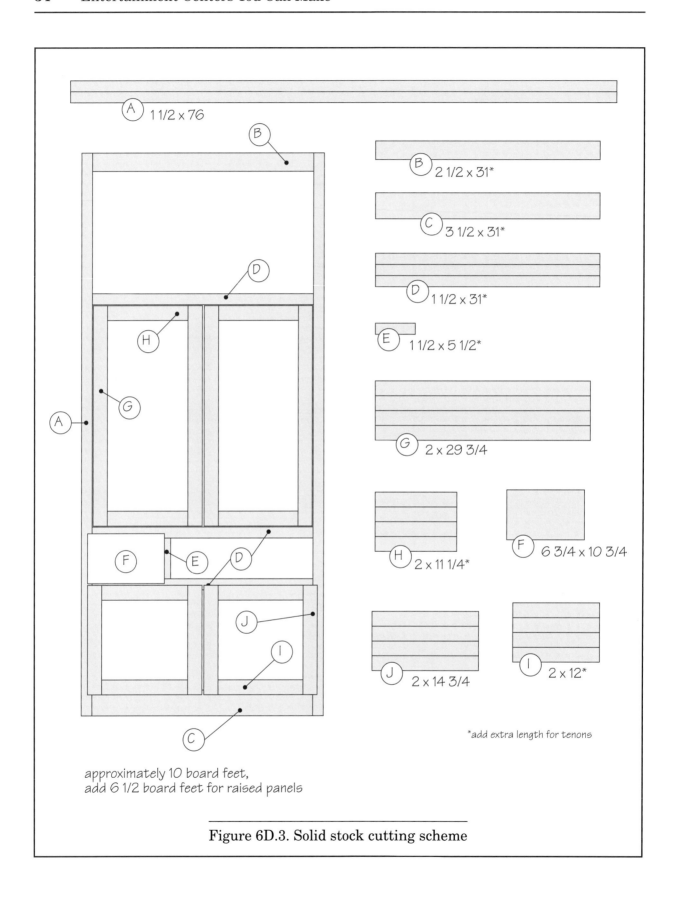

A  1 1/2 x 76

B  2 1/2 x 31*

C  3 1/2 x 31*

D  1 1/2 x 31*

E  1 1/2 x 5 1/2*

G  2 x 29 3/4

H  2 x 11 1/4*

F  6 3/4 x 10 3/4

J  2 x 14 3/4

I  2 x 12*

*add extra length for tenons

approximately 10 board feet,
add 6 1/2 board feet for raised panels

Figure 6D.3. Solid stock cutting scheme

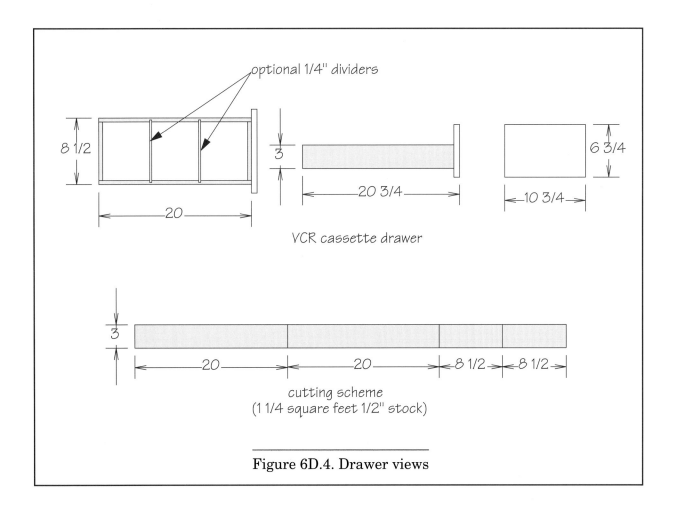

Figure 6D.4. Drawer views

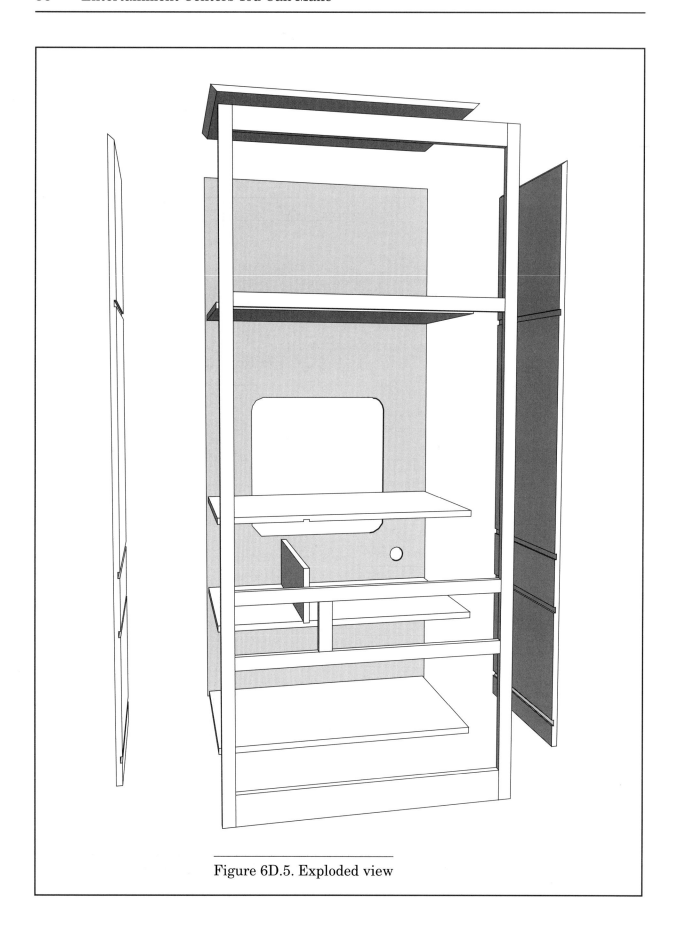

Figure 6D.5. Exploded view

## CABINET 6E: 39 X 54 X 24

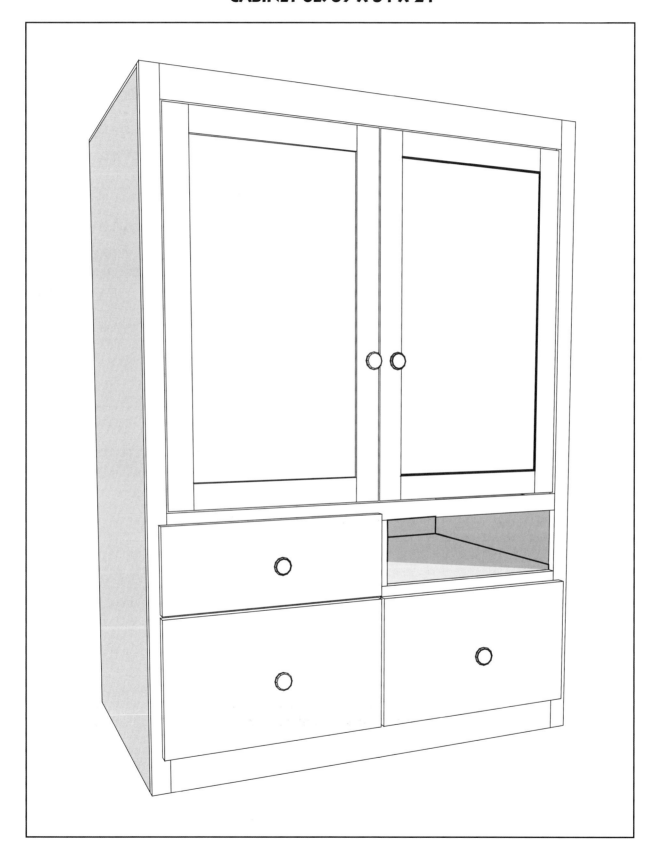

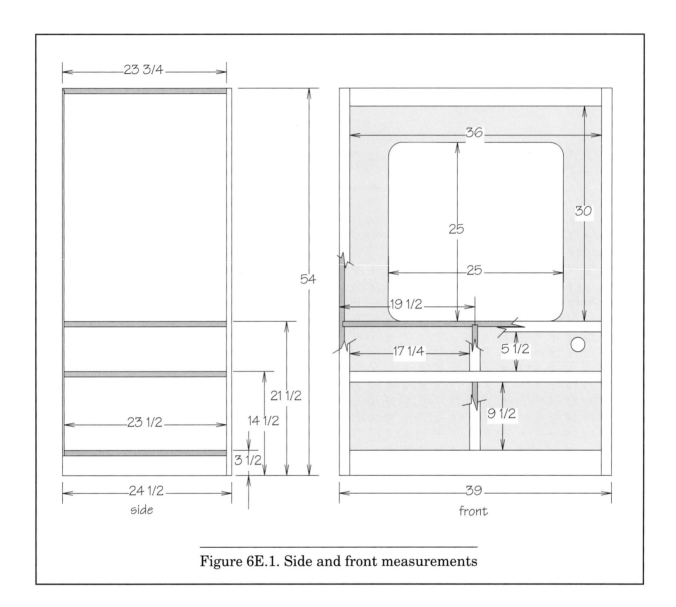

Figure 6E.1. Side and front measurements

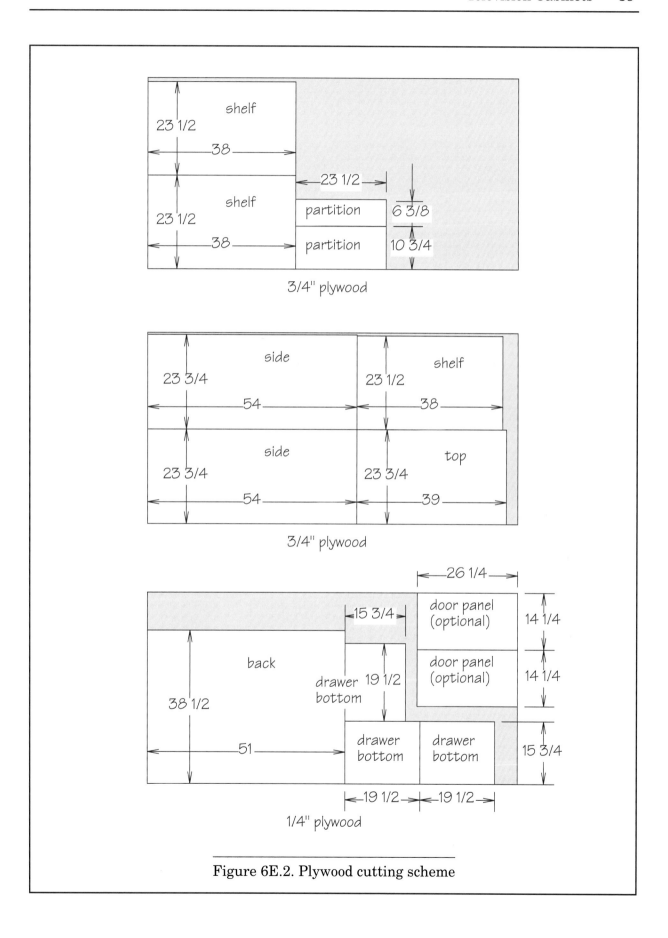

Figure 6E.2. Plywood cutting scheme

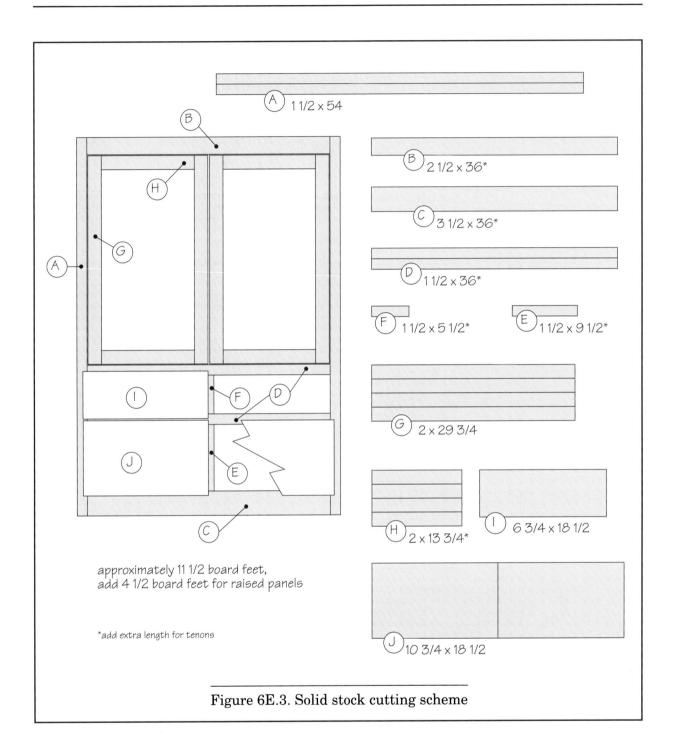

A ) 1 1/2 x 54

B ) 2 1/2 x 36*

C ) 3 1/2 x 36*

D ) 1 1/2 x 36*

F ) 1 1/2 x 5 1/2*

E ) 1 1/2 x 9 1/2*

G ) 2 x 29 3/4

H ) 2 x 13 3/4*

I ) 6 3/4 x 18 1/2

J ) 10 3/4 x 18 1/2

approximately 11 1/2 board feet,
add 4 1/2 board feet for raised panels

*add extra length for tenons

Figure 6E.3. Solid stock cutting scheme

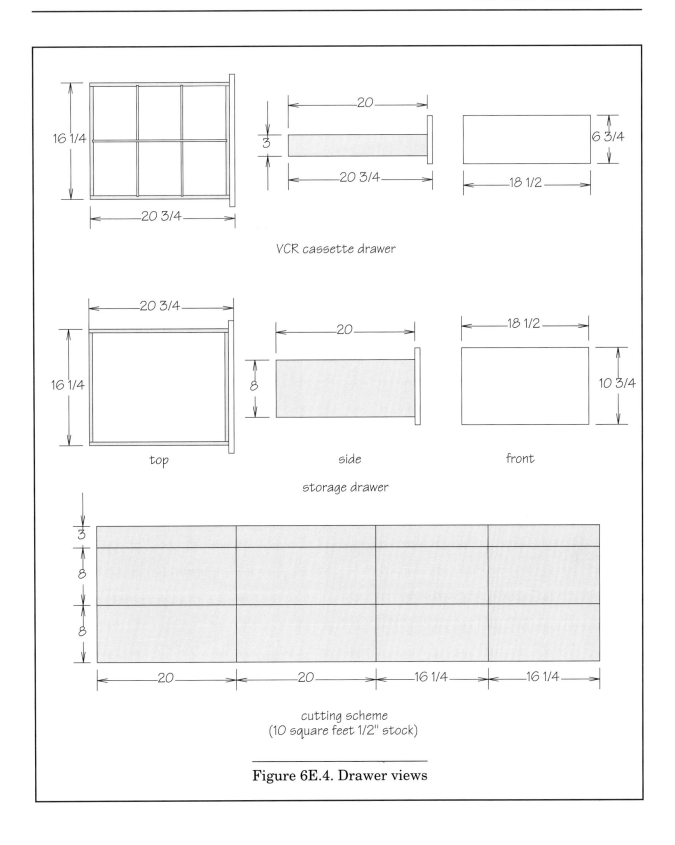

VCR cassette drawer

top          side          front

storage drawer

cutting scheme
(10 square feet 1/2" stock)

Figure 6E.4. Drawer views

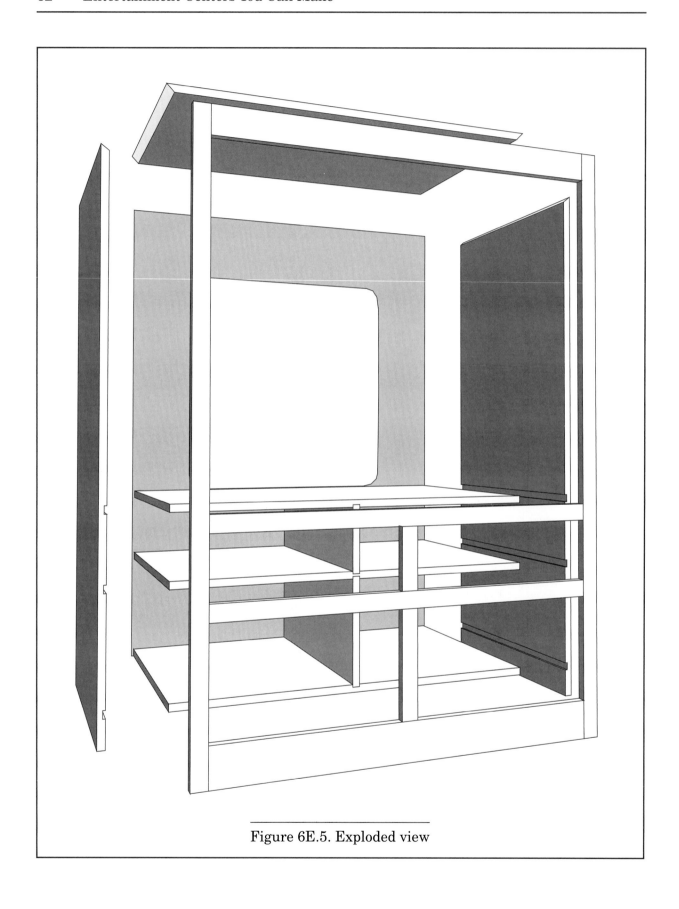

Figure 6E.5. Exploded view

## CABINET 6F: 39 X 58 X 24

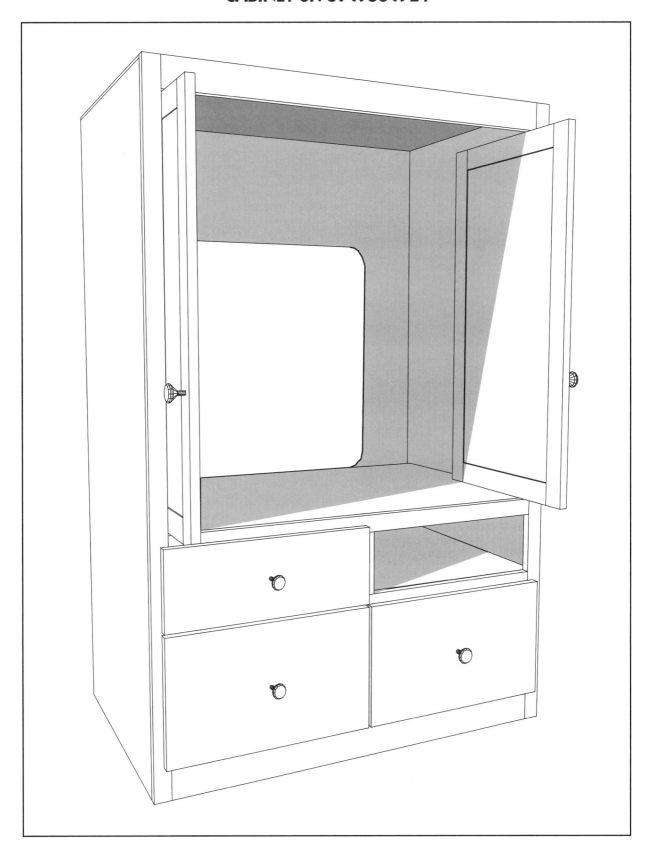

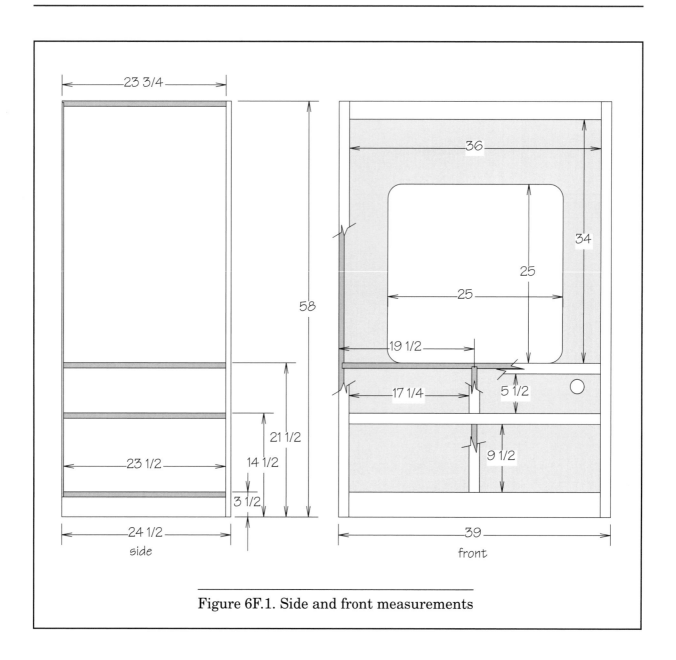

Figure 6F.1. Side and front measurements

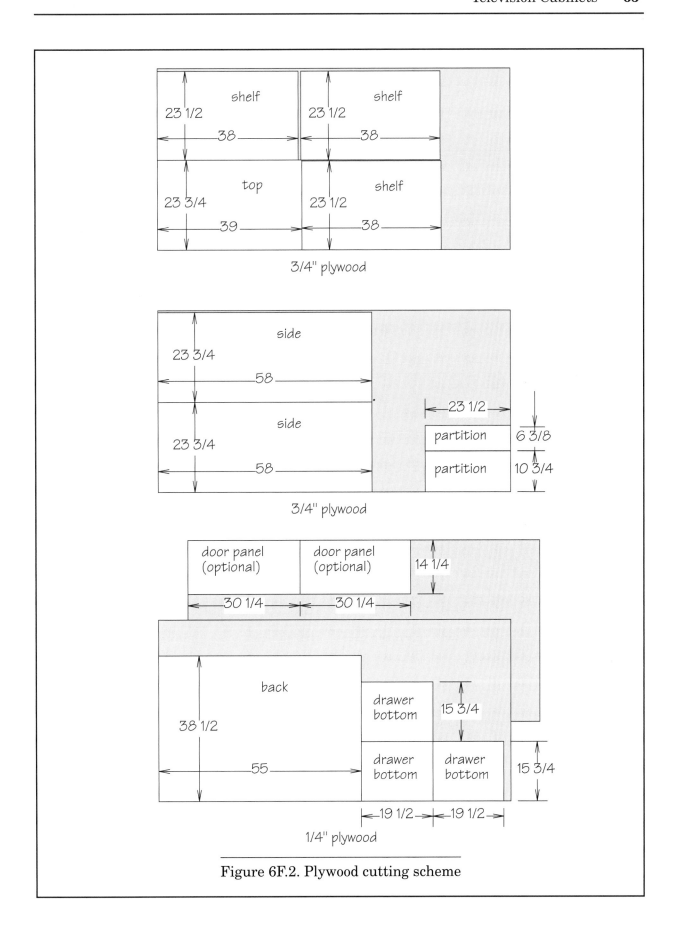

Figure 6F.2. Plywood cutting scheme

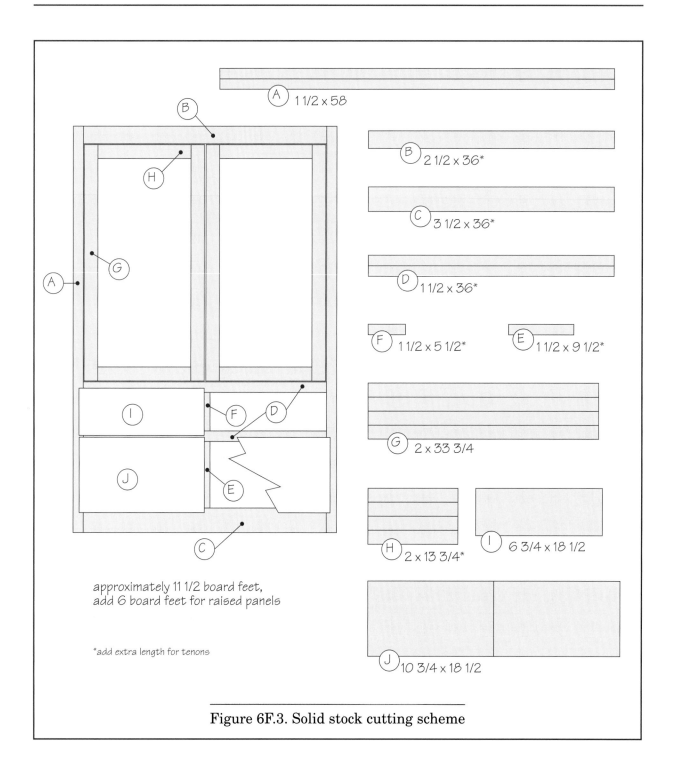

A  1 1/2 x 58

B  2 1/2 x 36*

C  3 1/2 x 36*

D  1 1/2 x 36*

F  1 1/2 x 5 1/2*          E  1 1/2 x 9 1/2*

G  2 x 33 3/4

H  2 x 13 3/4*          I  6 3/4 x 18 1/2

J  10 3/4 x 18 1/2

approximately 11 1/2 board feet,
add 6 board feet for raised panels

*add extra length for tenons

Figure 6F.3. Solid stock cutting scheme

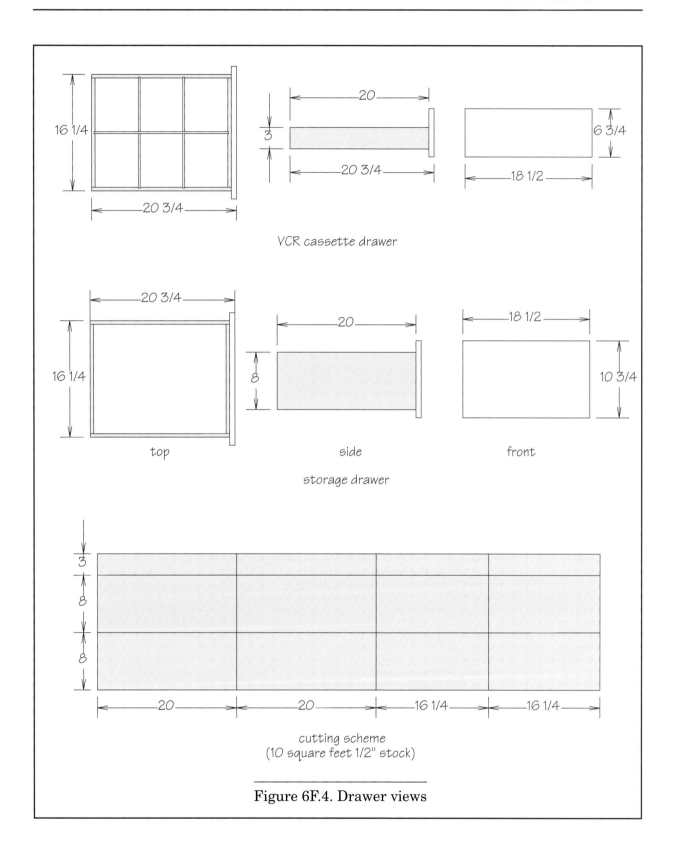

VCR cassette drawer

top                              side                              front

storage drawer

cutting scheme
(10 square feet 1/2" stock)

Figure 6F.4. Drawer views

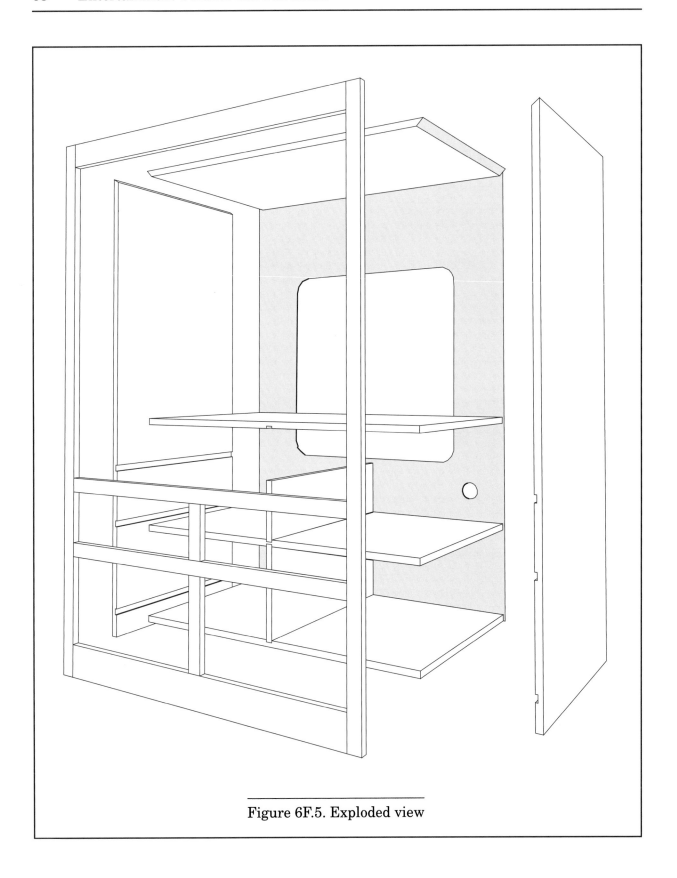

Figure 6F.5. Exploded view

## CABINET 6G: 39 X 72 X 24

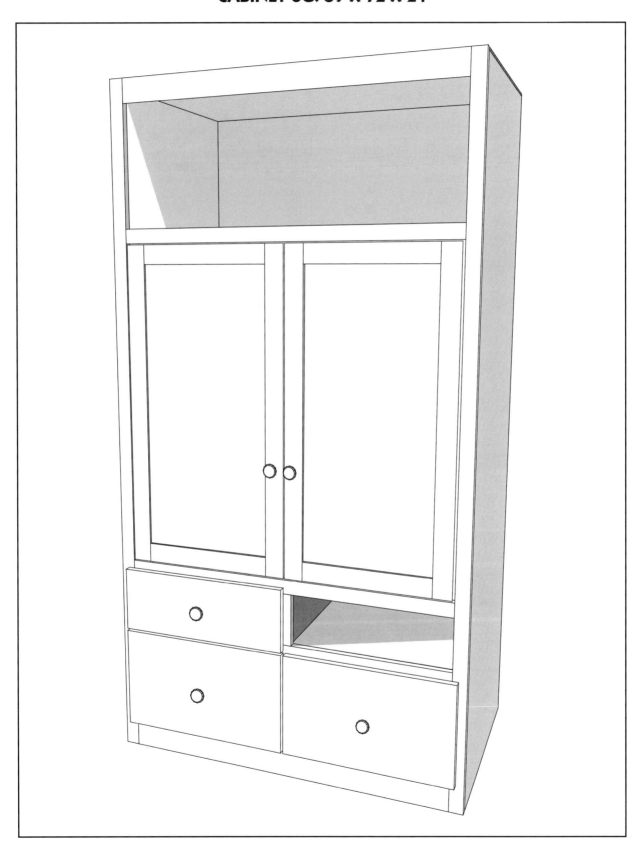

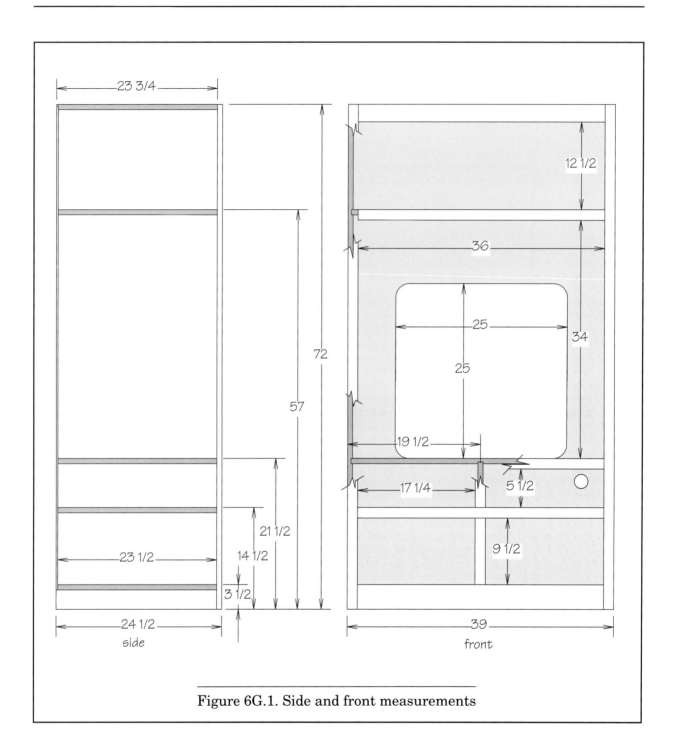

Figure 6G.1. Side and front measurements

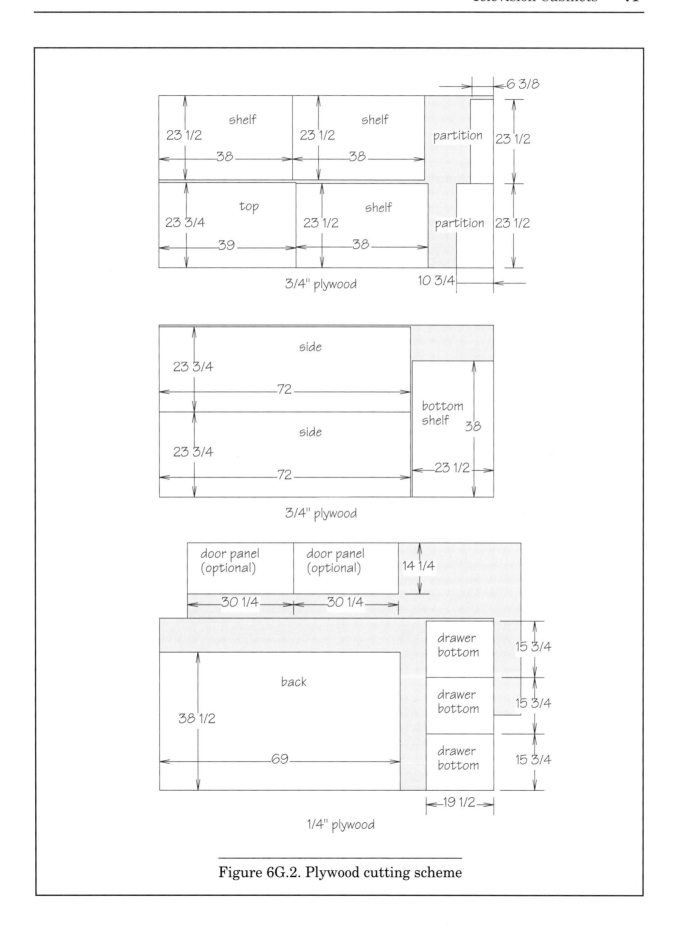

Figure 6G.2. Plywood cutting scheme

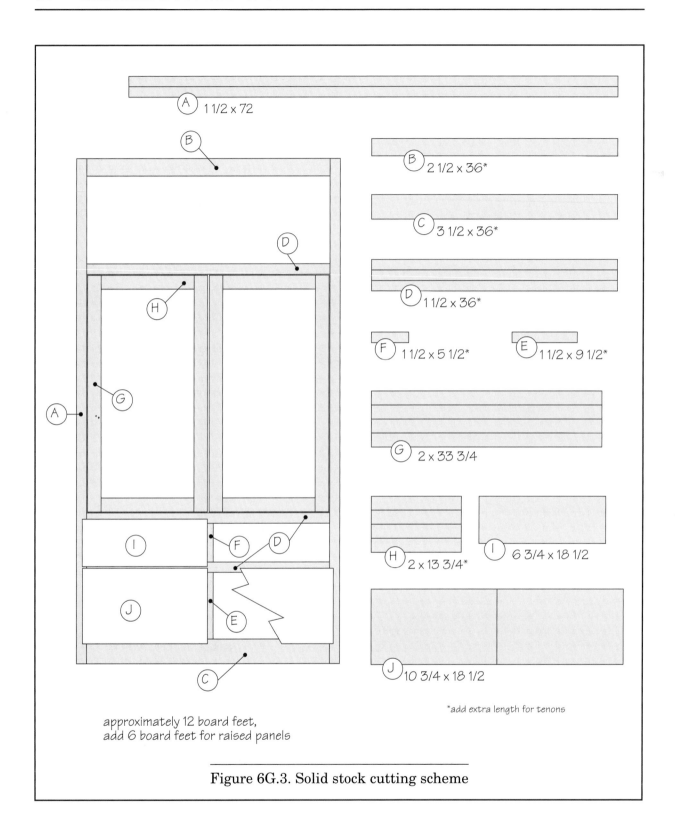

A    1 1/2 x 72

B    2 1/2 x 36*

C    3 1/2 x 36*

D    1 1/2 x 36*

F    1 1/2 x 5 1/2*        E    1 1/2 x 9 1/2*

G    2 x 33 3/4

H    2 x 13 3/4*        I    6 3/4 x 18 1/2

J    10 3/4 x 18 1/2

*add extra length for tenons

approximately 12 board feet,
add 6 board feet for raised panels

Figure 6G.3. Solid stock cutting scheme

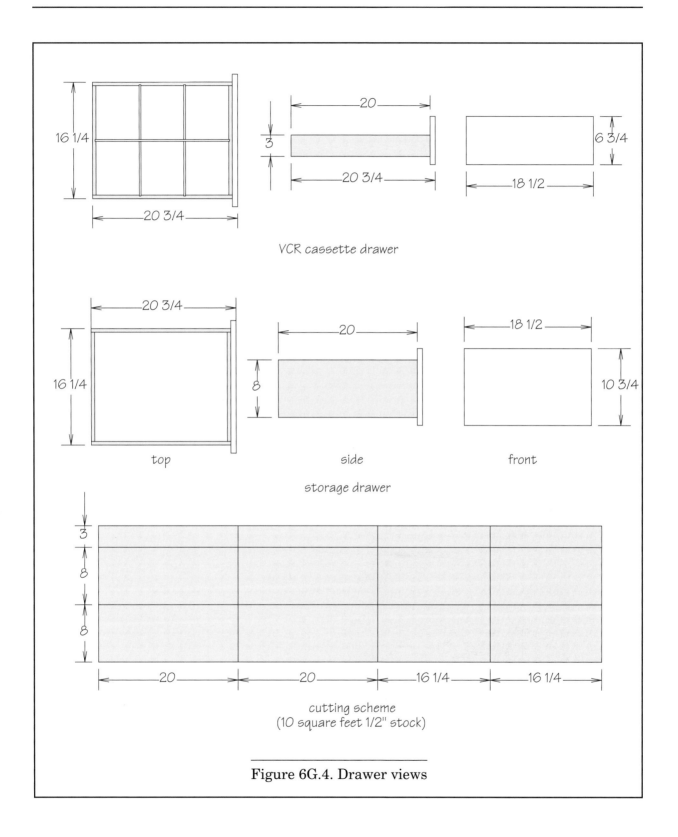

VCR cassette drawer

top                    side                    front

storage drawer

cutting scheme
(10 square feet 1/2" stock)

Figure 6G.4. Drawer views

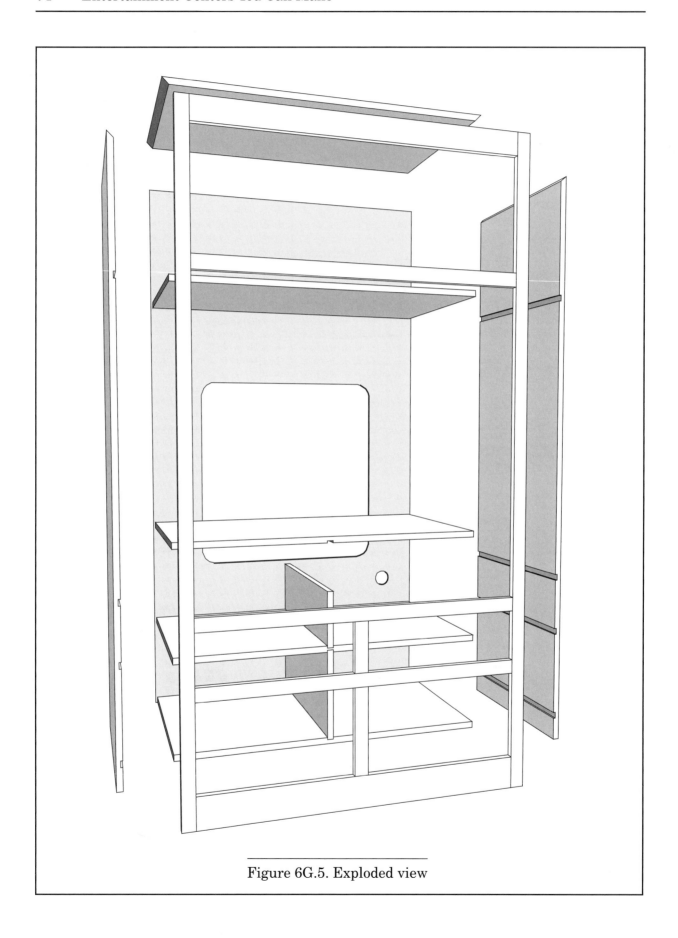

Figure 6G.5. Exploded view

## CABINET 6H: 39 X 76 X 24

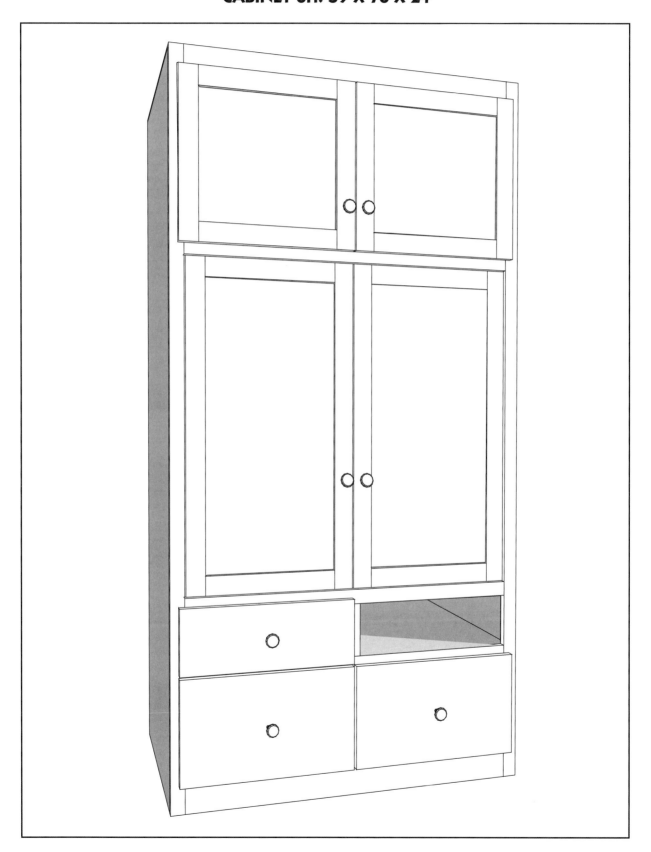

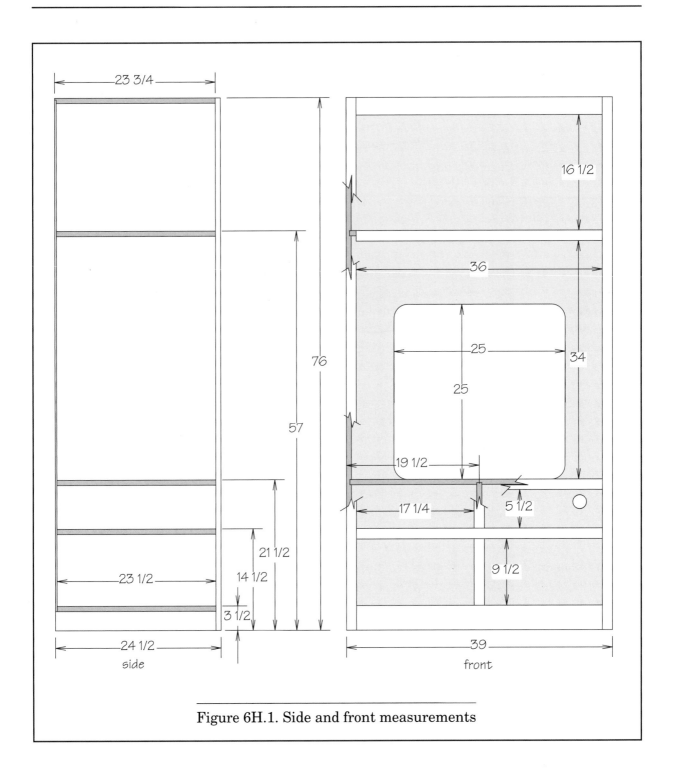

Figure 6H.1. Side and front measurements

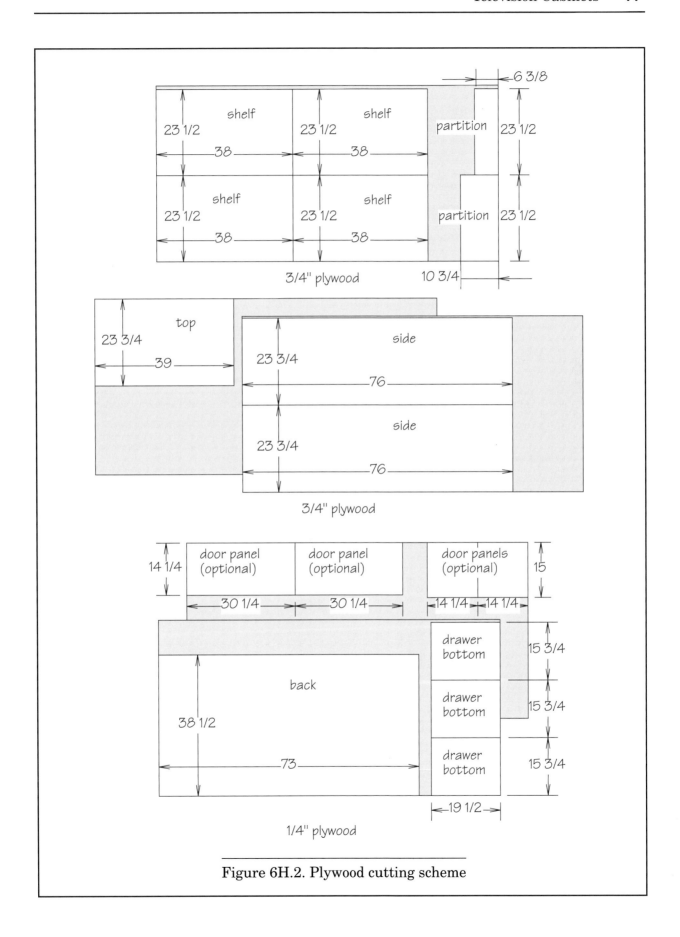

Figure 6H.2. Plywood cutting scheme

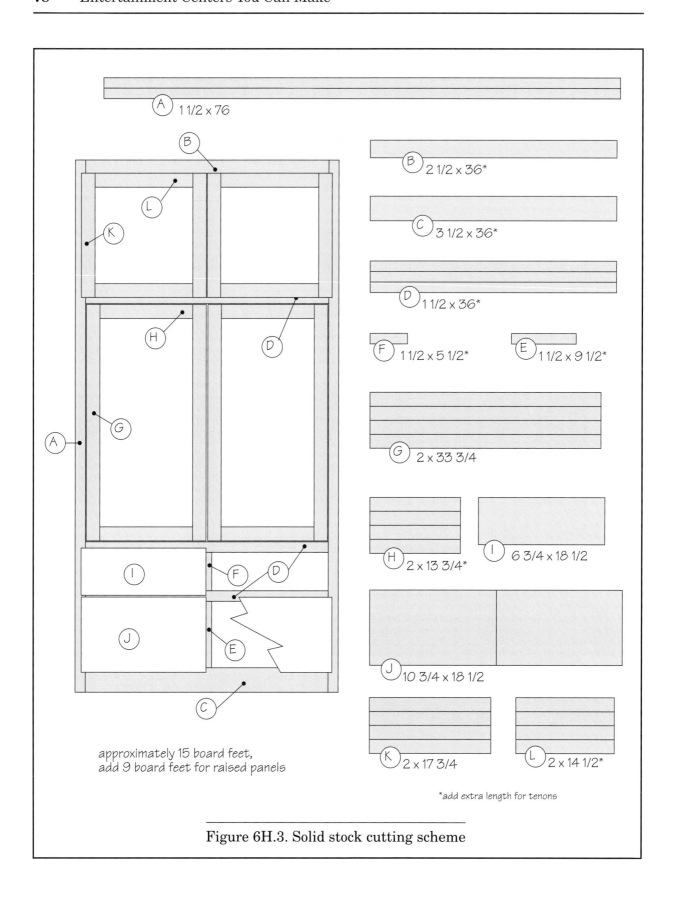

A    1 1/2 x 76

B    2 1/2 x 36*

C    3 1/2 x 36*

D    1 1/2 x 36*

F    1 1/2 x 5 1/2*

E    1 1/2 x 9 1/2*

G    2 x 33 3/4

H    2 x 13 3/4*

I    6 3/4 x 18 1/2

J    10 3/4 x 18 1/2

K    2 x 17 3/4

L    2 x 14 1/2*

approximately 15 board feet,
add 9 board feet for raised panels

*add extra length for tenons

Figure 6H.3. Solid stock cutting scheme

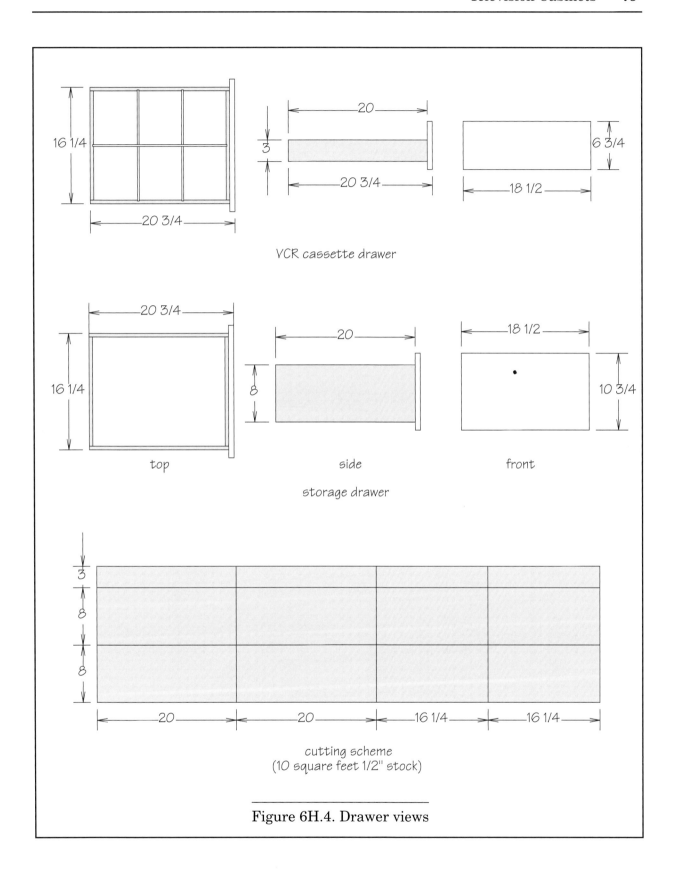

Figure 6H.4. Drawer views

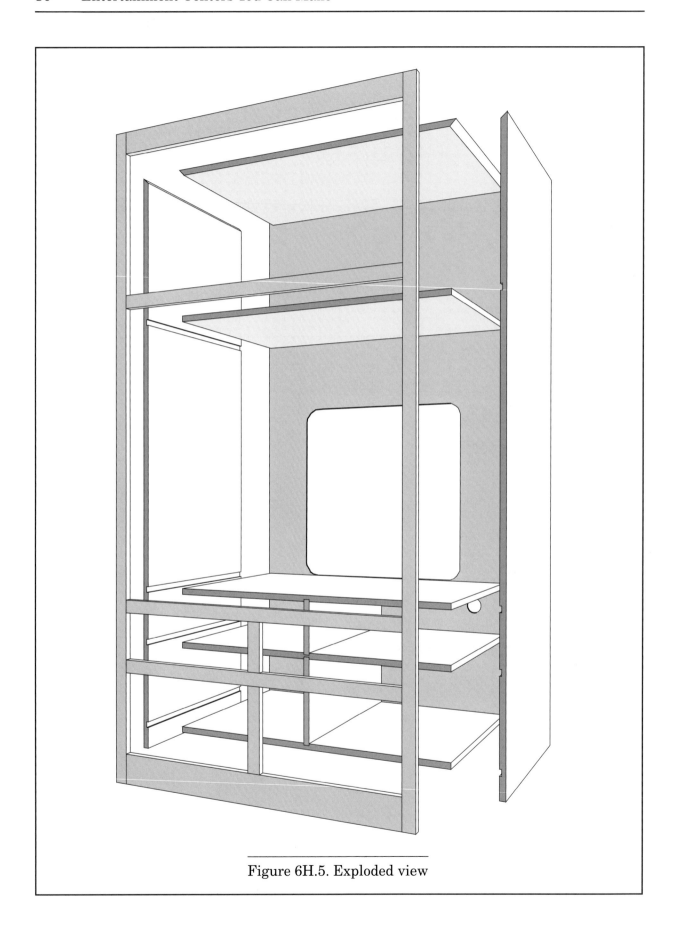

Figure 6H.5. Exploded view

# · Chapter 7 ·

# SIDE CABINETS

The four side cabinets are numbered 7A through 7D and come in two heights, 54 and 72 inches, and two depths, 16 and 21 inches. All of them are 20 inches wide (Figure 7.1). Cabinets of both depths will accommodate almost all standard home audio components. The two depths offer a wider variety of options. Many of the possible configurations are illustrated in chapter 5. Although the intended purpose of one or more of the side towers is to flank a television cabinet, a single cabinet can also stand alone as an audio tower.

Like the television cabinets, the side cabinets have backs of 1/4-inch plywood. The drawings illustrate a 1-inch slot down the center of the back through which to run cords and cables. The slots can be made wider if necessary or eliminated if unneeded (if the cabinet will be used entirely for display or storage).

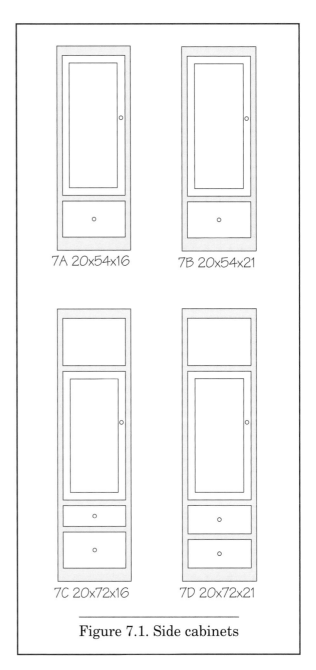

7A 20x54x16     7B 20x54x21

7C 20x72x16     7D 20x72x21

Figure 7.1. Side cabinets

## CABINET 7A: 20 X 54 X 16

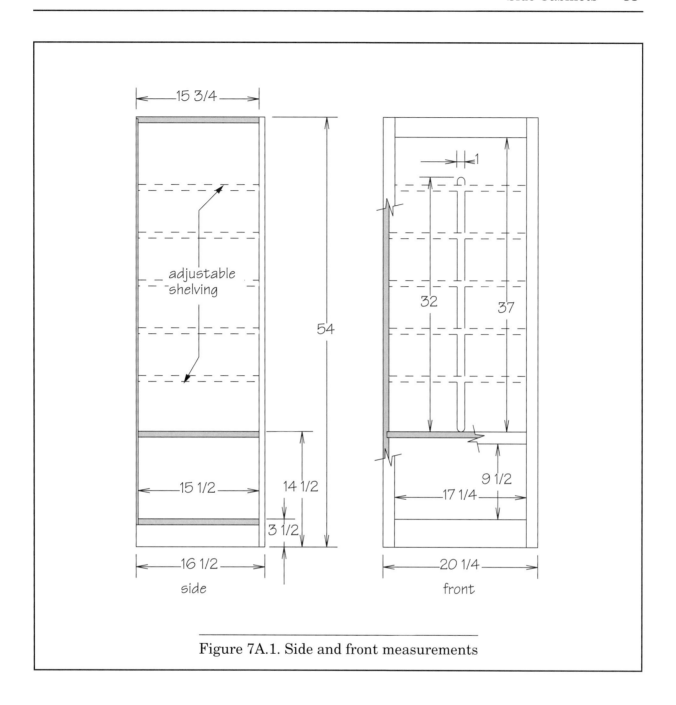

Figure 7A.1. Side and front measurements

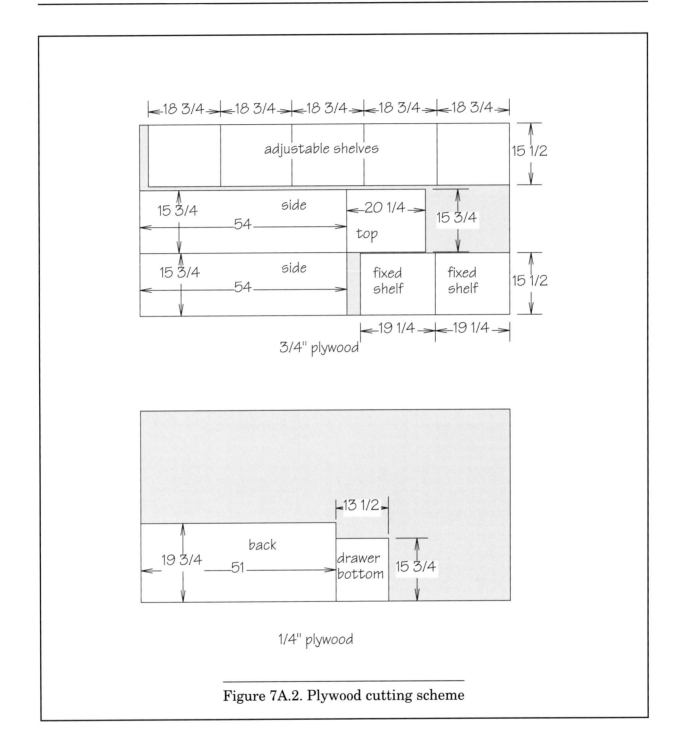

Figure 7A.2. Plywood cutting scheme

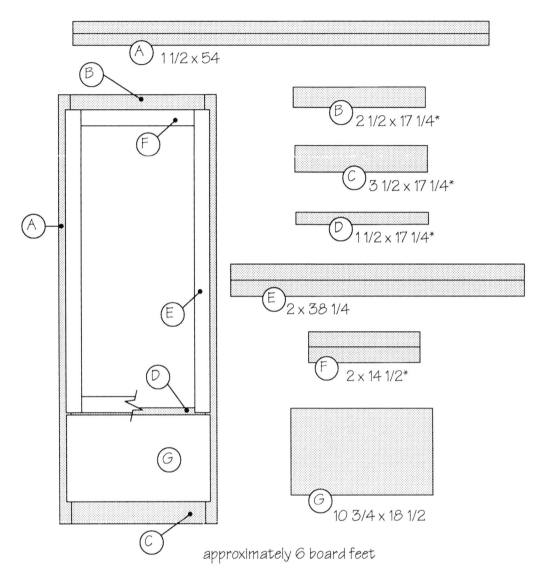

Ⓐ 1 1/2 x 54

Ⓑ 2 1/2 x 17 1/4*

Ⓒ 3 1/2 x 17 1/4*

Ⓓ 1 1/2 x 17 1/4*

Ⓔ 2 x 38 1/4

Ⓕ 2 x 14 1/2*

Ⓖ 10 3/4 x 18 1/2

approximately 6 board feet

*add extra length for tenons

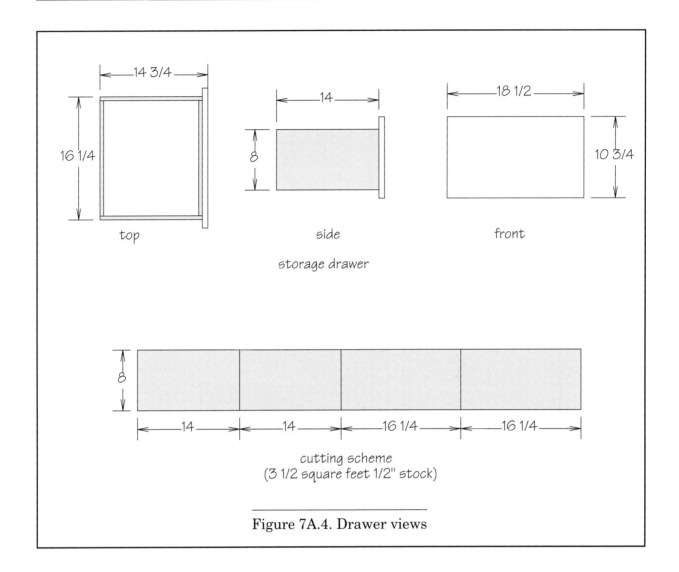

top

side

front

storage drawer

cutting scheme
(3 1/2 square feet 1/2" stock)

Figure 7A.4. Drawer views

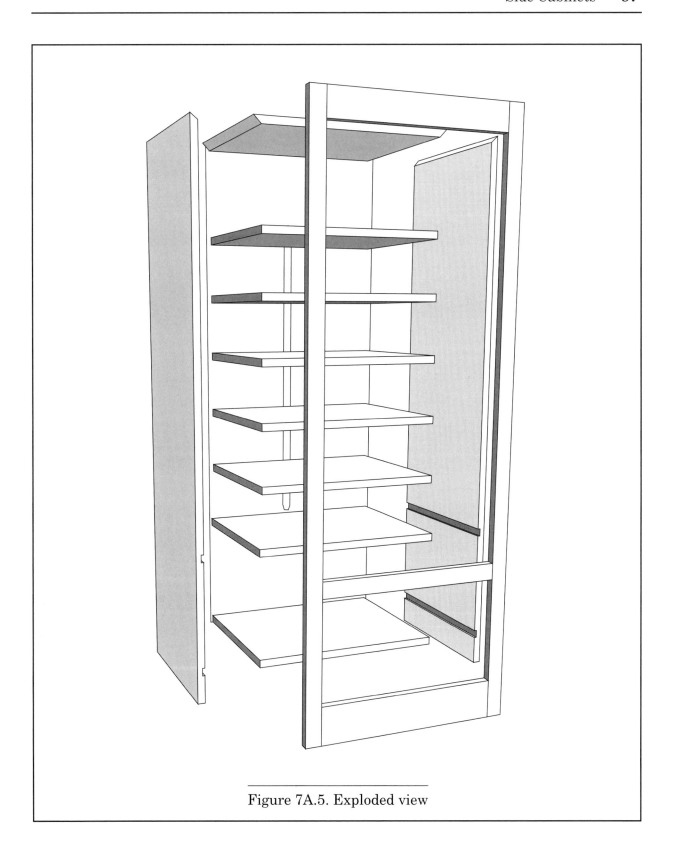

Figure 7A.5. Exploded view

## CABINET 7B: 20 X 54 X 21

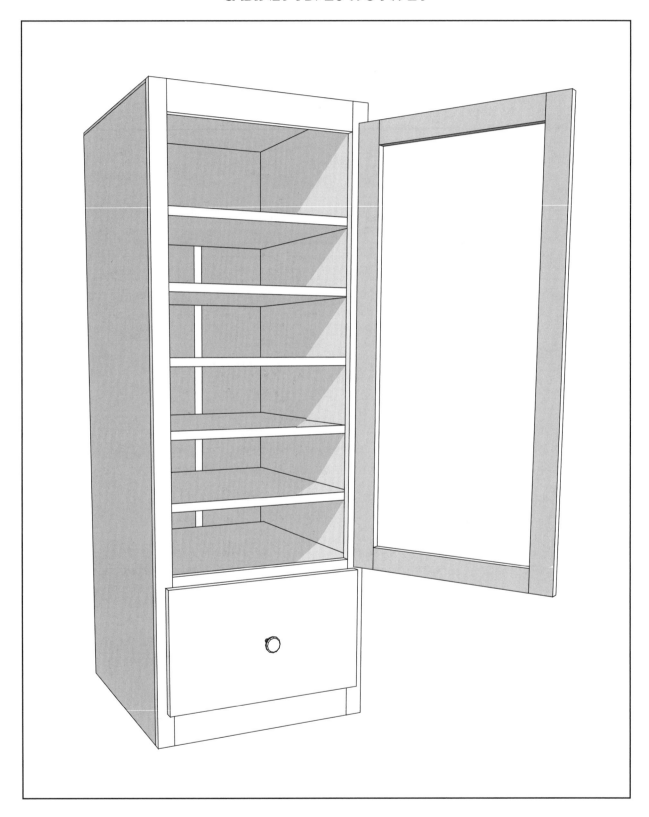

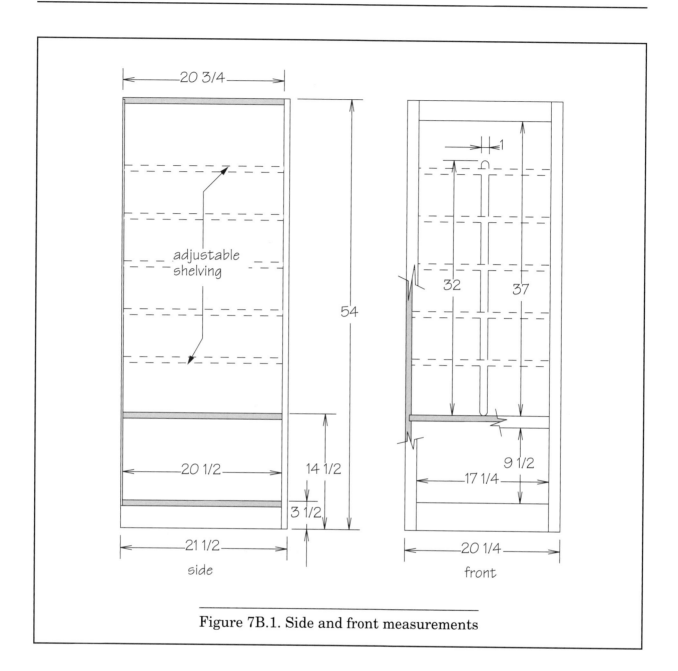

Figure 7B.1. Side and front measurements

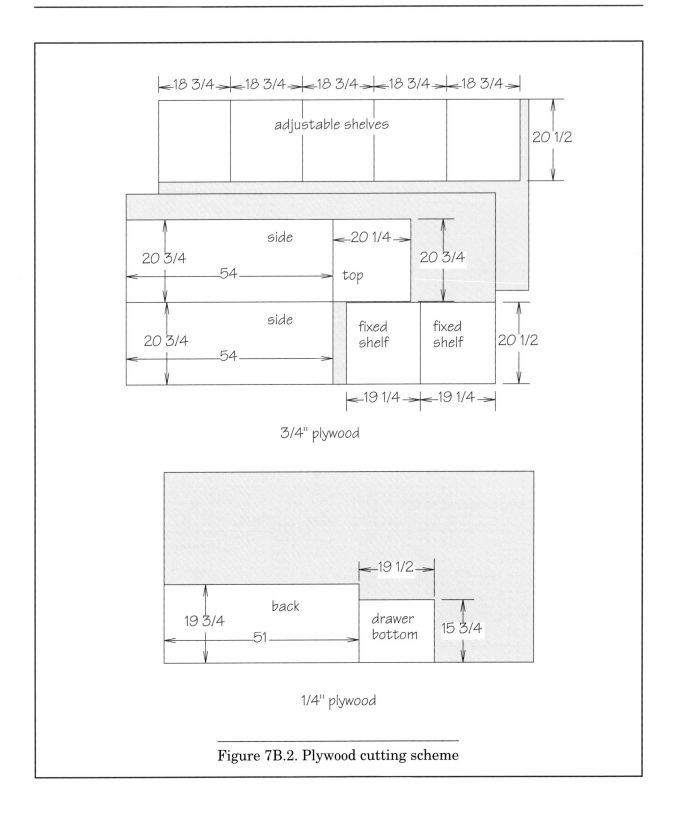

Figure 7B.2. Plywood cutting scheme

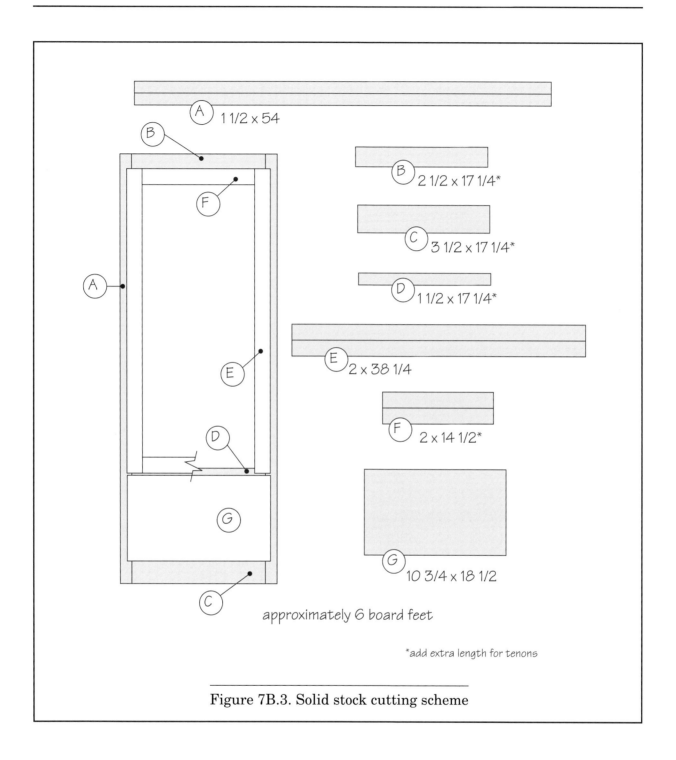

A  1 1/2 x 54

B  2 1/2 x 17 1/4*

C  3 1/2 x 17 1/4*

D  1 1/2 x 17 1/4*

E  2 x 38 1/4

F  2 x 14 1/2*

G  10 3/4 x 18 1/2

approximately 6 board feet

*add extra length for tenons

Figure 7B.3. Solid stock cutting scheme

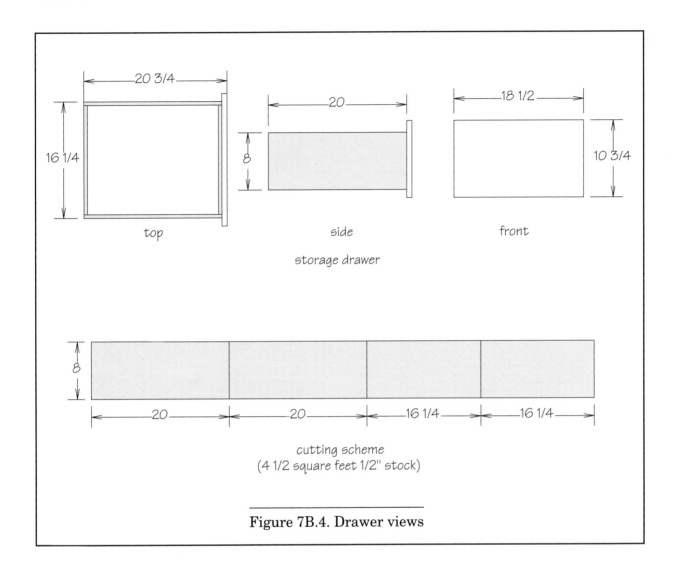

top

side

front

storage drawer

cutting scheme
(4 1/2 square feet 1/2" stock)

**Figure 7B.4. Drawer views**

Figure 7B.5. Exploded view

## CABINET 7C: 20 X 72 X 16

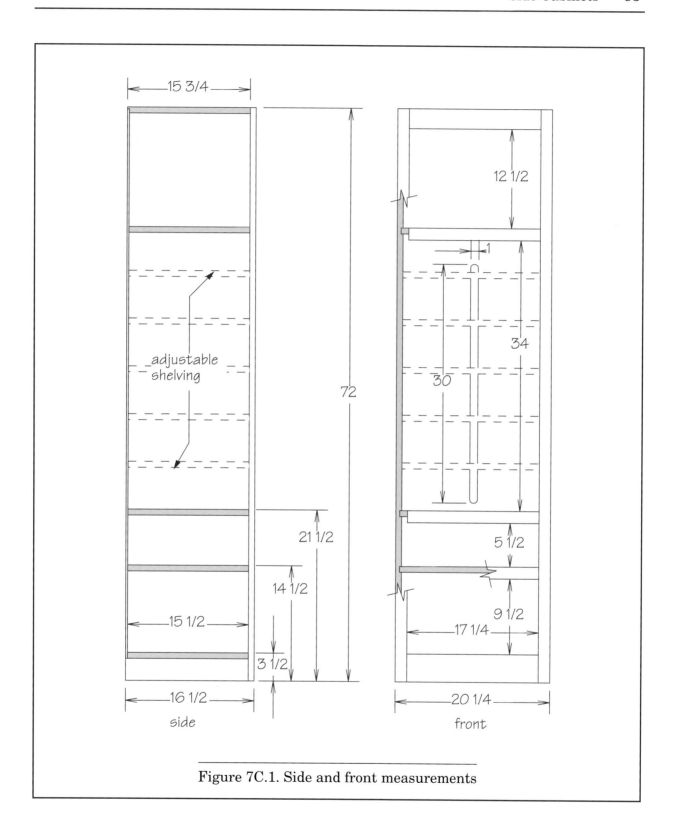

Figure 7C.1. Side and front measurements

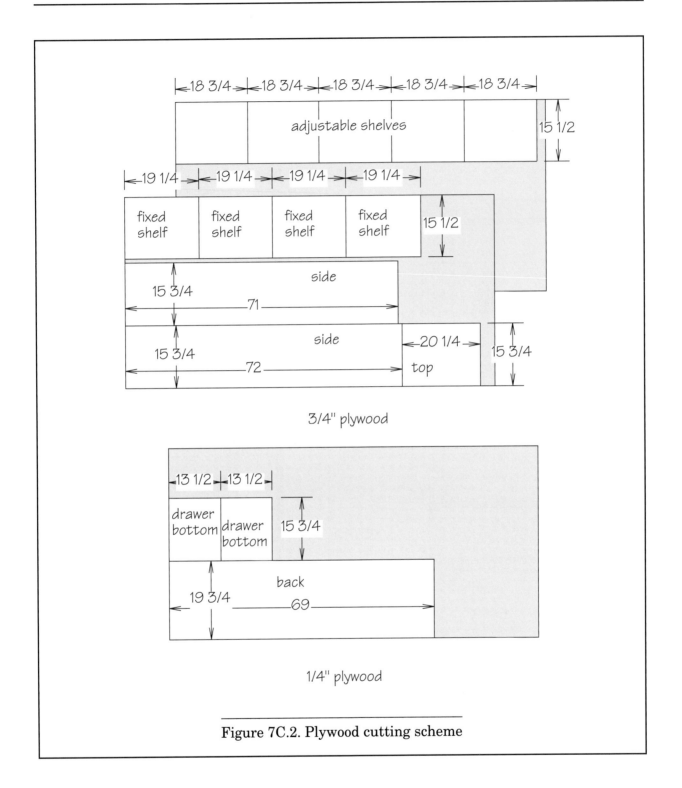

Figure 7C.2. Plywood cutting scheme

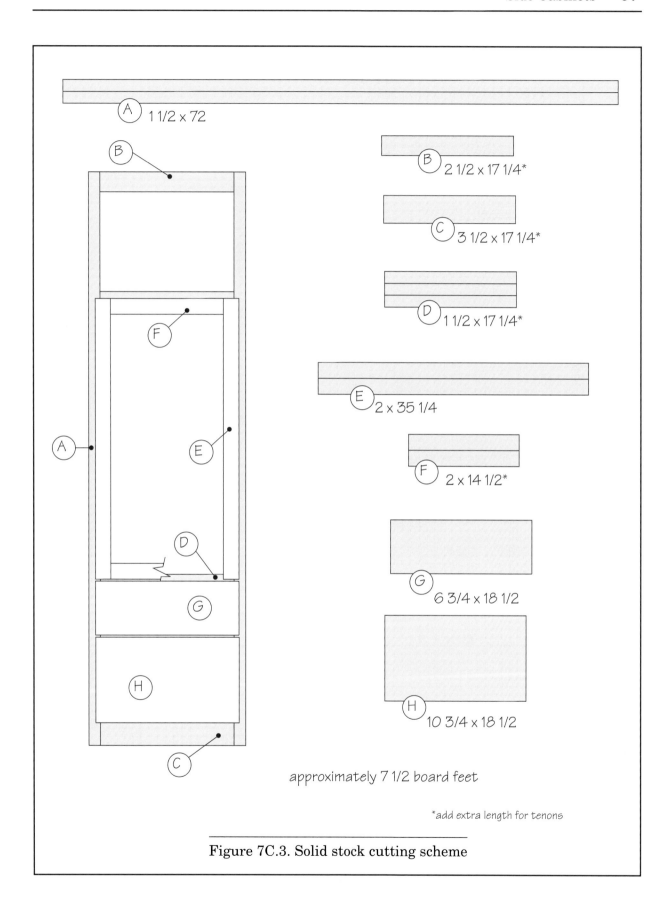

A 1 1/2 x 72

B 2 1/2 x 17 1/4*

C 3 1/2 x 17 1/4*

D 1 1/2 x 17 1/4*

E 2 x 35 1/4

F 2 x 14 1/2*

G 6 3/4 x 18 1/2

H 10 3/4 x 18 1/2

approximately 7 1/2 board feet

*add extra length for tenons

Figure 7C.3. Solid stock cutting scheme

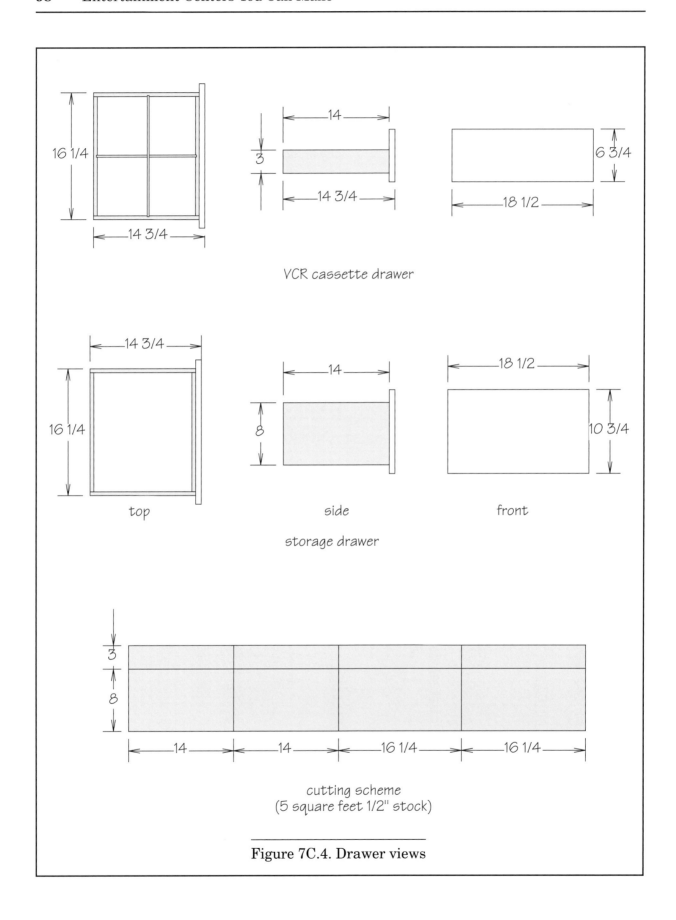

VCR cassette drawer

top                         side                        front

storage drawer

cutting scheme
(5 square feet 1/2" stock)

Figure 7C.4. Drawer views

Figure 7C.5. Exploded view

## CABINET 7D: 20 X 72 X 21

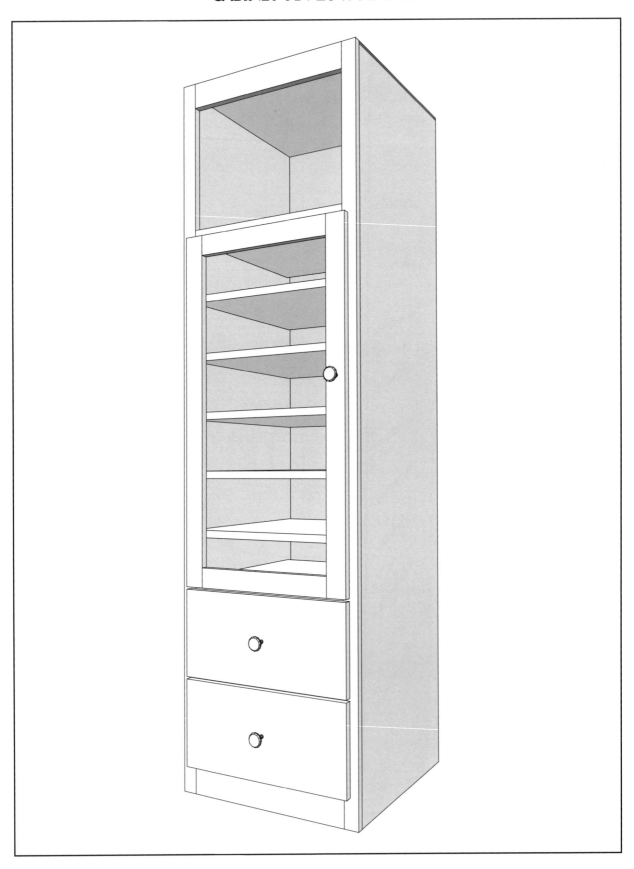

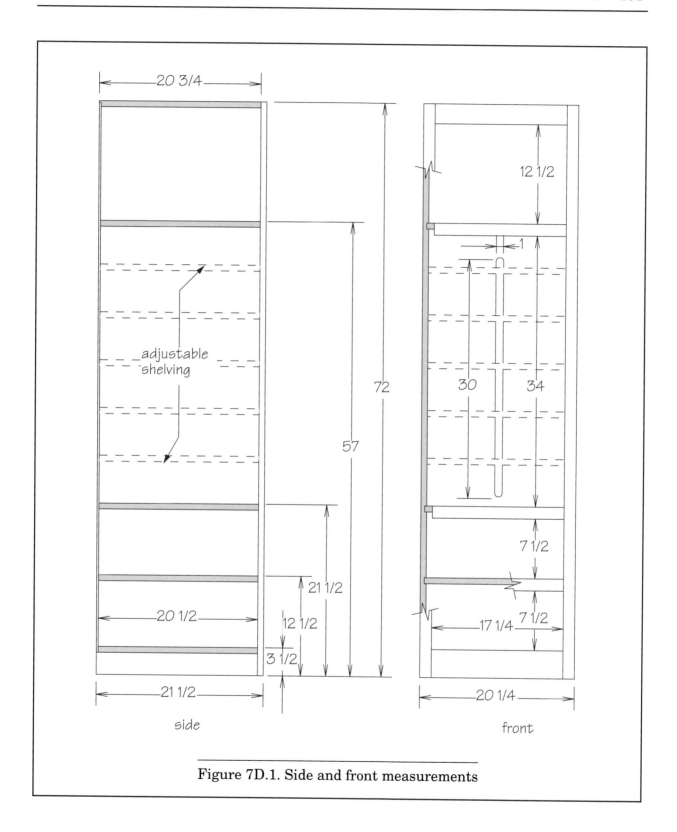

Figure 7D.1. Side and front measurements

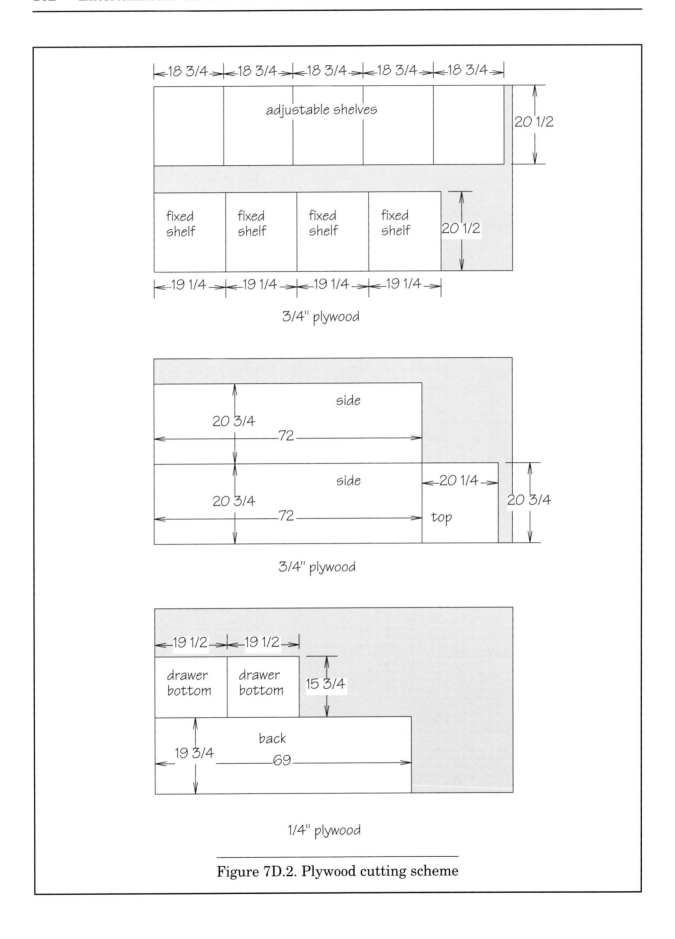

Figure 7D.2. Plywood cutting scheme

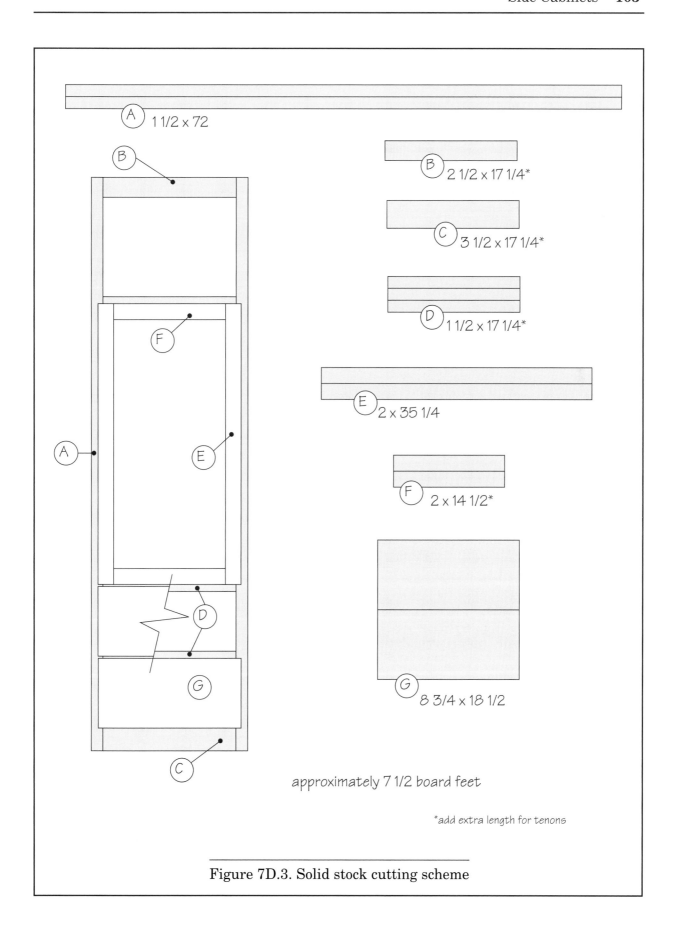

(A) 1 1/2 x 72

(B) 2 1/2 x 17 1/4*

(C) 3 1/2 x 17 1/4*

(D) 1 1/2 x 17 1/4*

(E) 2 x 35 1/4

(F) 2 x 14 1/2*

(G) 8 3/4 x 18 1/2

approximately 7 1/2 board feet

*add extra length for tenons

Figure 7D.3. Solid stock cutting scheme

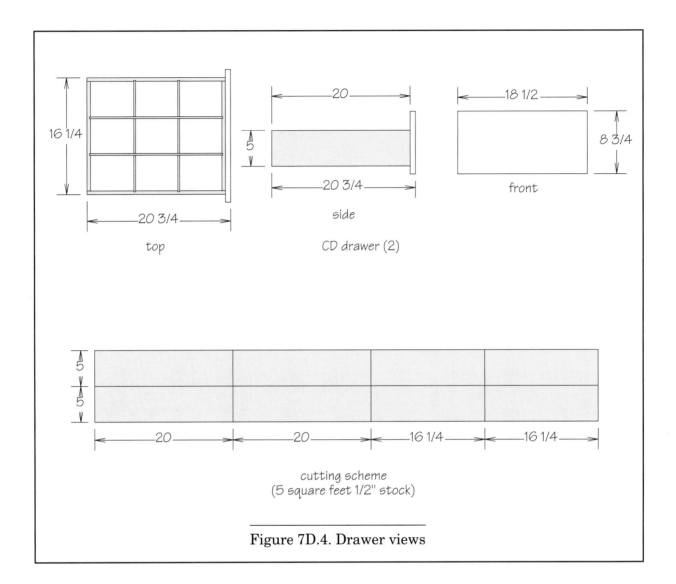

16 1/4

20 3/4

top

20

5

20 3/4

side

CD drawer (2)

18 1/2

8 3/4

front

5

5

20    20    16 1/4    16 1/4

cutting scheme
(5 square feet 1/2" stock)

Figure 7D.4. Drawer views

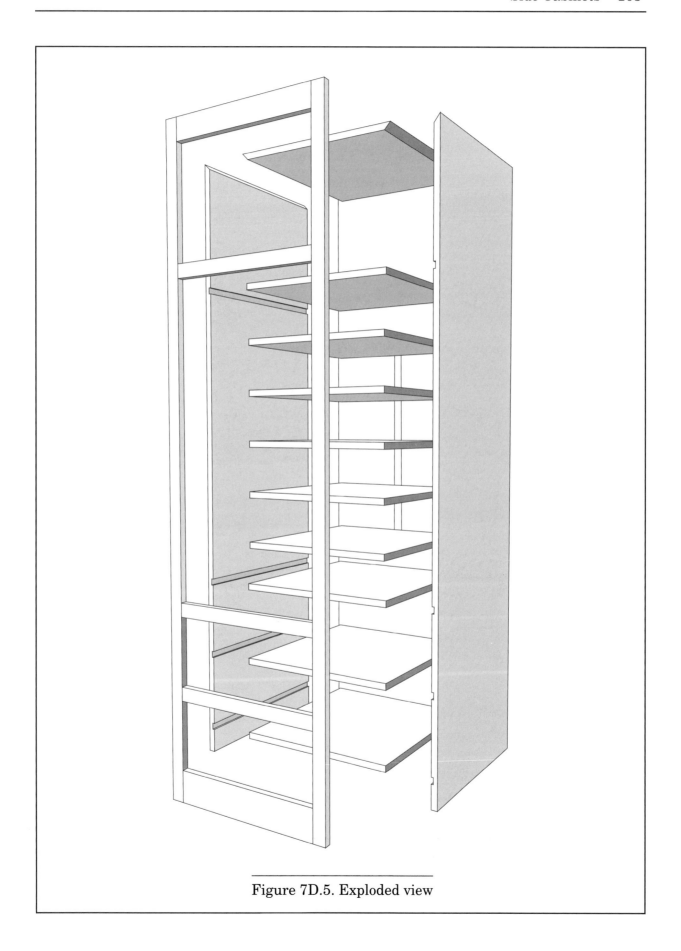

Figure 7D.5. Exploded view

# • Chapter 8 •

# ASSEMBLY

**B**efore cutting any of the plywood pieces, it's very important to understand the relationships between the top and sides of each cabinet and between the cabinets you have chosen for your ensemble. How you join the pieces depends on the overall configuration of the entertainment center and how you plan to finish off the top (discussed in chapter 9). Note that the lengths for the tops and sides given in the plywood cutting schemes in chapters 6 and 7 are overall. Before cutting the pieces, make the necessary adjustments to each length.

## CHOOSING YOUR JOINERY METHOD

The goal is to conceal the plywood edges that run along the joint from front to back. The method you select will depend on the individual cabinet and its placement in the ensemble.

Figure 8.1 shows four different procedures:

• Figure 8.1A is a miter joint, which has a continuous grain pattern up the side and across the top. This is a tricky cut to make on a wide piece of plywood. Both pieces must be cut precisely to yield a flawless joint. You would use this joint on an exposed edge.

• Figure 8.1B shows a rabbeted top with an optional edge band. This joint provides a continuous grain pattern across the top. You would use this joint without the edge band on a side cabinet where it will

abut the television cabinet (and therefore be unexposed) and on both sides of the television cabinet if it's flush with the top and face of the side cabinets. You would also use this method all the way around if you planned to trim the top with any kind of molding. Use the edge band (applied before the rabbet is cut) on exposed edges.

• Figure 8.1C illustrates a rabbeted side with optional edge band. Use the veneer edge band if you want a continuous grain pattern up the sides but where the small strip of cross grain along the top is insignificant. Use this joint without the edge band if the finish of the top is of no consequence—that is, if any crown molding or valence would subsequently conceal the top. Also, the rabbet can be cut in the sides with the same setup you'd use to make the dadoes for the remaining fixed shelves.

• Figure 8.1D shows how to join the top to the side with a piece of 1×1 solid stock biscuited to each. The cross grain will show equally across both planes, and the edge can be rounded over once the face frame has been applied. Do not use nails to secure this piece, or router damage and personal injury may occur. Apply the piece to the sides first.

## CABINET

Cut all the plywood pieces at one time and mark them according to their position and orientation in the cabinet. Put the fixed

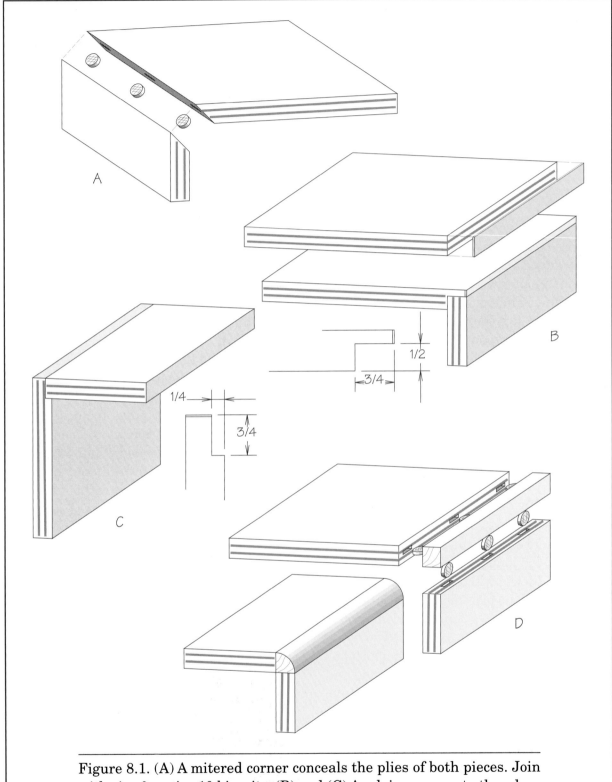

Figure 8.1. (A) A mitered corner conceals the plies of both pieces. Join with size 0 or size 10 biscuits. (B) and (C) Applying veneer to the edges is easy, and only a small strip of cross grain will show along the adjoining surface. (D) Using a piece of 1×1 solid stock for the edge allows for rounding over if desired. Caution: Do not use nails to attach this piece!

shelves aside; apply edge bands where needed to the top or sides and make the necessary cuts as described in Figure 8.1.

The cabinet back fits into a rabbet cut into the back edges of the sides and top. You can make the rabbets before or after assembling the cabinet proper. Use a router or a table saw fixed with a dado blade to make the cut before assembly. Just remember to stop the cut 1/4 inch from the top of the side pieces (Figure 8.2). Otherwise a small hole will show where the top and the sides meet at the back corner.

Note: If you use the joint described in Figure 8.1D, wait until you've cut the rabbets in the side before applying the 1×1.

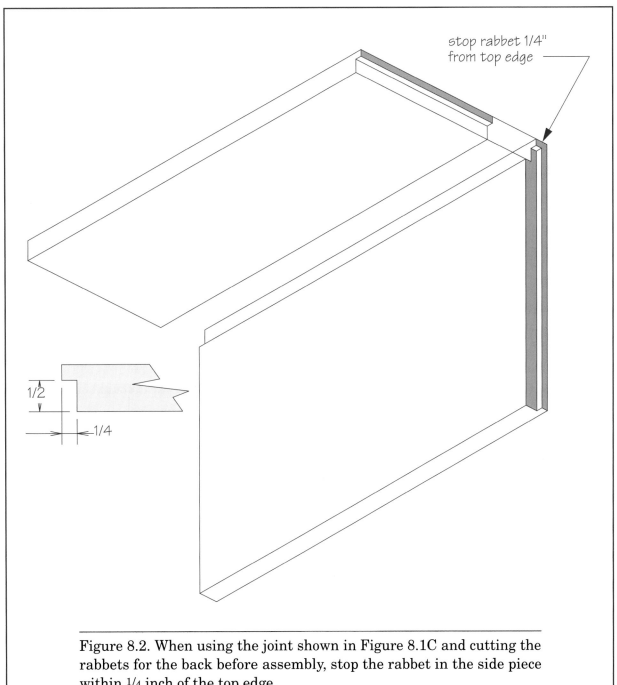

Figure 8.2. When using the joint shown in Figure 8.1C and cutting the rabbets for the back before assembly, stop the rabbet in the side piece within 1/4 inch of the top edge.

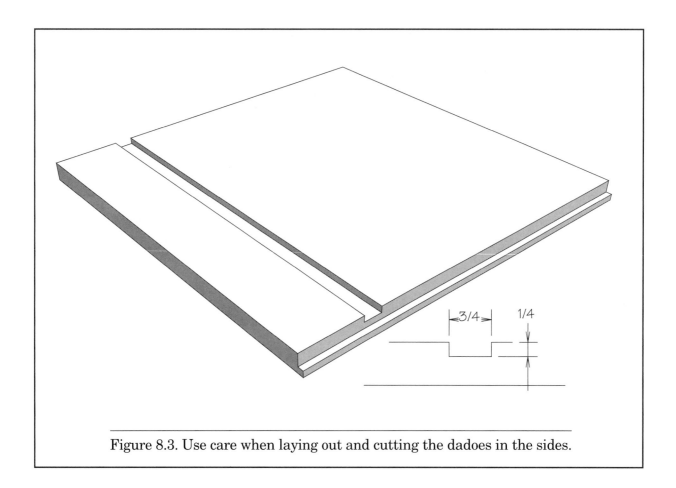

Figure 8.3. Use care when laying out and cutting the dadoes in the sides.

Using a rabbeting bit *after* assembly will require that you jump over the fixed shelves, leaving some stock uncut. Remove this excess stock with a chisel. The back panels are dimensioned to fit into a rabbet that is 1/2 inch wide. A 3/8-inch rabbet, however, is sufficient if that's the size bit you have.

Place the sides inside up on the bench, and carefully lay out the dadoes for the fixed shelves (other than the top), as shown in Figure 8.3. Accuracy in laying out and cutting the 1/4-inch-deep dadoes is important, as the dadoes will determine the placement of the shelves. Use a router run against a straight edge clamped to the stock. Use a 3/4-inch bit for MDF and a 23/32-inch bit for 3/4-inch plywood (see chapter 1).

When laying out and cutting the dadoes, be consistent. If you measure up from the bottom edge of the side to the top surface of the shelf on one side, do the same thing on the other side. Check the fit of the shelves in their dadoes before proceeding.

Next, lay out and cut the dadoes in the shelves that will receive the dividers between the VCR compartment and drawer and the two drawers in the base of the television cabinet.

You will likely want to install adjustable shelving in the side cabinets and possibly the television cabinet (see chapter 3). Now is the time to make the preparations, before you have everything put together.

To save yourself some time later, thoroughly sand the inside faces of all the pieces before assembling them.

There is no best way to assemble the pieces, but the job will be much easier with the help of a second pair of hands and plenty of bar clamps. Brush glue into the dadoes and rabbets prior to assembly. Before the glue has had time to set, check to make sure that the front edges of all the pieces are flush and that the cabinet is square (Figure 8.4). Clean up any squeeze-out before the glue has fully set.

In lieu of clamps you can use 4d or 6d nails to hold the pieces together while the glue dries. Set the nail heads below the surface. Keep in mind, however, that even when filled, the nail holes will be notice-able and might detract from the overall appearance of the piece. Do not use nails along the top edge if you will later round it over.

Cut the backs from 1/4-inch panel stock and check the fit with the cabinet. The radius for the corners is arbitrary (I often use a can of wood filler or jar lid as a pattern for a corner radius). If using a jigsaw to make the cut, do so with the back of the plywood facing up to minimize tear-out on the front, finished side. Sand the edges smooth.

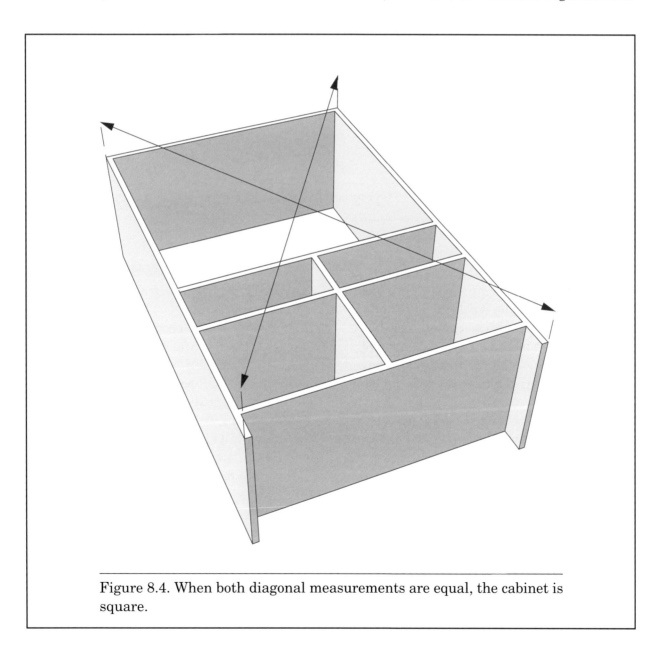

Figure 8.4. When both diagonal measurements are equal, the cabinet is square.

Also lay out and cut the hole through which the VCR cable and power cord will pass—approximately 2 inches in diameter. Don't forget to check the position of the hole so that you don't inadvertently cut it on the wrong side (easy to do if the back side is up). If you use a drill or hole saw to make the cut, do so from the front, also to minimize tear-out. The backs for the side cabinets have 1-inch slots through which will run cords and cables.

With the cabinet lying facedown, brush glue into the rabbet cuts and along the back edges of the shelves. Be sparing with the glue because squeeze-out will be hard to get rid of. Lay the back in place on the cabinet. Check again that the pieces are squared up before fastening the back in place with 3/4-inch brads or small staples.

## FACE FRAME

Rip the pieces for the face frame to the widths shown in the solid stock cutting schemes (Figures 6A–H.3 and 7A–D.3). When cutting the pieces to length, remember to add at least 1/2 inch for 1/4-inch stub

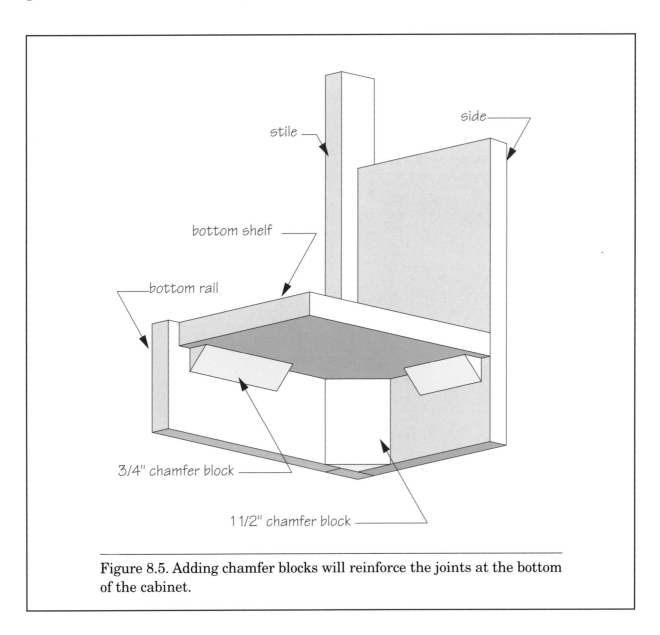

Figure 8.5. Adding chamfer blocks will reinforce the joints at the bottom of the cabinet.

tenons on the pieces specified if you choose that method of joinery.

You can follow one of two procedures for fitting the face frame to the cabinet. One is to preassemble the face frame and attach it as a unit; the other is to fit one piece at a time to the cabinet.

With the first method, the top and bottom rails—at the very least—are joined to the stiles with either stub tenons or biscuits. Intermediate rails and stiles, which at 1½ inches are too narrow to be joined effectively with biscuits, can be tenoned. Otherwise, they can be installed later in the same manner as described in the second method. If you have tenoned the short stiles (on the television cabinet), fit them to their respective rails first. Then fit the rails to the long stiles. The short stiles are centered on their dividers. All joints, of course, are glued before they are assembled. Set the frame aside to dry, but first make sure all corners

are square. Use biscuits or 6d nails and glue to hold the frame to the cabinet.

For a piece-by-piece assembly in which all joints are butted, begin by fastening the stiles to the sides with biscuits or 6d nails and glue. The rails are individually cut to fit between the stiles. Attach them to the shelves in the same manner as the stiles, making sure the corners are square. The short stiles, which are centered on their dividers, are then fit between their respective rails.

Figure 8.5 shows how to reinforce the joints between the bottom rail and the stiles and along the bottom shelf. Also install any necessary mounting blocks for casters (described in chapter 9).

Using the cutting schemes in the selected drawings, assemble the doors and drawers according to the method of your choice, as covered in Part I. Chapter 9 gives additional options.

# ▪ Chapter 9 ▪

# VARIATIONS, OPTIONS, AND IDEAS

The individual components for the entertainment centers presented in this book are by design simple in nature and method of assembly. As you've discovered, there are many ways to combine the components into an attractive and functional entertainment center. The simplicity of design, however, also is the key to adding stylistic depth and visual interest, thus transforming something common into something unique.

What follows are some options and ideas to help you get the most out of building and enjoying your entertainment center.

## GLIDES, CASTERS, AND LEVELERS

Any cabinet that isn't permanently built in will be moved around once in a while. Heavy cabinets will be dragged across the floor, which is not good for the floor or the cabinet, especially those with plywood sides where the veneer can be torn away.

It's a good idea to add some sort of feet to protect the floor and facilitate moving. A variety of glides and casters are available either locally or by catalog. Where ease of movement is wanted, use casters. Figure 9.1 shows a typical plate-type swivel caster as it would be mounted to a cabinet (pin-type casters are not recommended). Notice the 3/4-inch mounting block glued and screwed to the bottom side of the shelf. Most plate casters are 2 3/4 inches tall and will fit nicely beneath the cabinet. Mounted as shown, a

set of four will raise the cabinet 3/4 inch above the floor. If your entertainment center will sit on thick carpeting, increase the thickness of the mounting blocks.

Mounting levelers to the cabinet bottoms will help when it comes time to set up your entertainment center in its final resting place. This is especially important when two or more tall cabinets are grouped together. Floors that are even slightly out of level will transmit the discrepancy and exaggerate it at the top of the grouping. If you choose to use mechanical levelers, which are also readily available, be sure that they are sturdy enough to carry the intended load and that they will withstand lateral movement should you ever slide the cabinet across the floor.

## DOORS AND DRAWERS

To some extent, doors and drawers are optional and sometimes interchangeable items. Take, for example, television cabinet 6B. Although the drawings call for doors on the lower part of the cabinet, drawers can easily be installed instead. It's a simple matter to install a partition and additional stile into the cavity. Then you can build drawers to suit.

Doors can be left off altogether for display purposes. This is especially true in the upper cavities of the television cabinets. Compare cabinets 6D and 6H. Just because a particular drawing shows—or does not

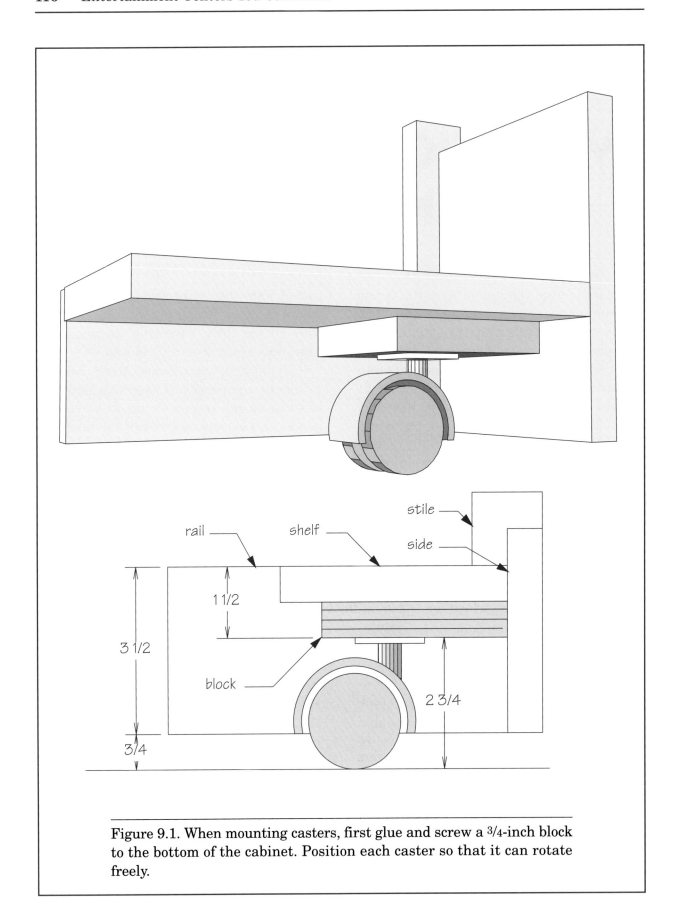

Figure 9.1. When mounting casters, first glue and screw a 3/4-inch block to the bottom of the cabinet. Position each caster so that it can rotate freely.

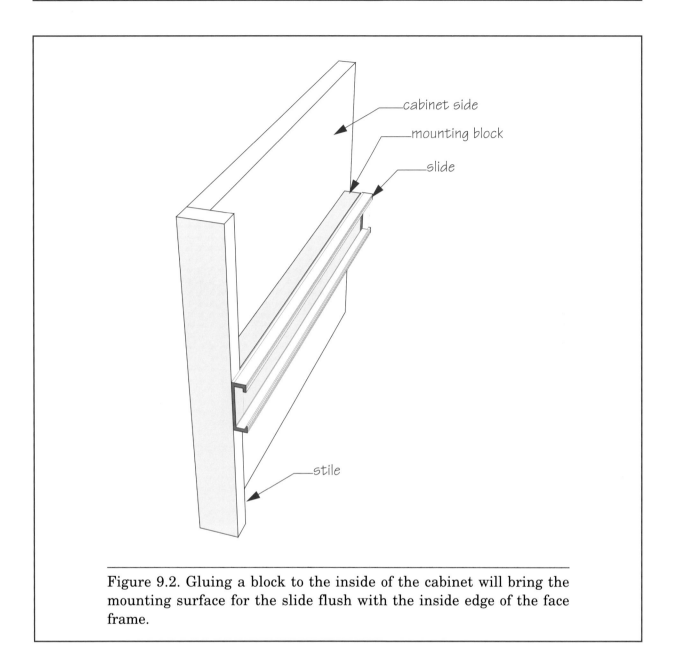

Figure 9.2. Gluing a block to the inside of the cabinet will bring the mounting surface for the slide flush with the inside edge of the face frame.

show—doors doesn't mean you have to follow it to the letter.

In short cavities, such as the 9½-inch lower cavity of television cabinets, drawers are preferable to doors. The space is too limited to be generally useful for display.

Both the lower and upper cavities in the television cabinets and the side cabinets are perfect spots for speakers, however. You can use speakers right off the shelf or mount your own to custom fit the openings.

Speaker-cover fabric is commercially available. You can stretch the fabric over door frames and conceal the speakers behind hinged doors for easy access. Alternatively, you can make a frame that will fit neatly into the opening.

## Clearances and Slides

Flipper doors fit inside the face frame and are flush with the frame when closed. Dimensions given for the frame components

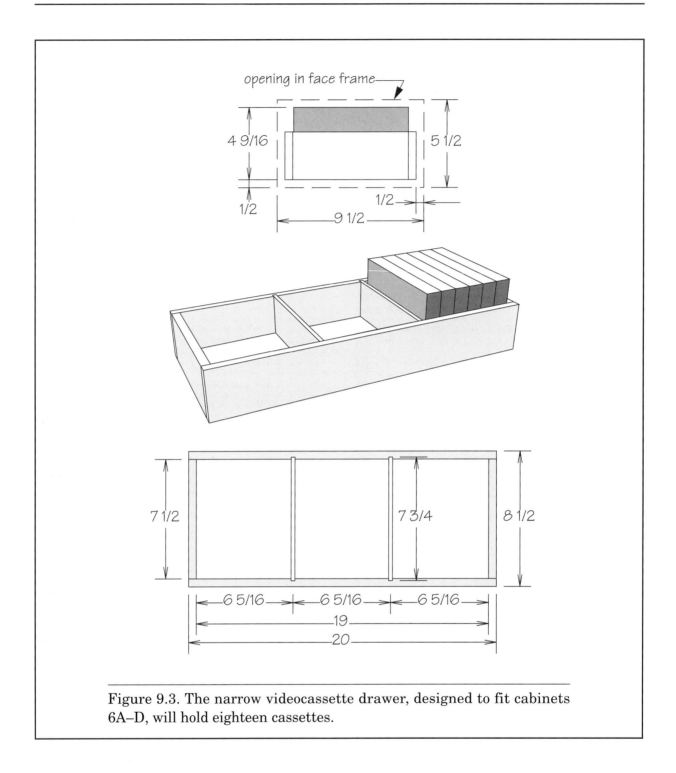

Figure 9.3. The narrow videocassette drawer, designed to fit cabinets 6A–D, will hold eighteen cassettes.

allow for 1/8-inch clearance on the top and bottom and a little more than 1/8 inch on either side and between the two doors.

The overlay doors and applied drawer fronts are dimensioned to be 1¼ inches larger than their openings from top to bot-

tom and side to side. That is, they overlay the face frames by 5/8 inch all the way around. This allows for a space of 1/4 inch between adjacent doors and drawers.

The drawers are dimensioned to give 1/2-inch clearance on each side and on the bottom. This will accommodate most commercial slides, such as Accuride. Also, most slides are designed for attachment directly to the cabinet side (Euro-style), but you can purchase adapters for face-frame installation. An alternative is to attach a piece of 3/4-inch stock at least 2 inches wide to the cabinet side. This will bring the slide flush with the inside edge of the face frame (Figure 9.2). Use glue and two 11/4-inch screws to hold the block securely.

## Videocassettes and Compact Disks

With careful study of the plans, you'll notice that several of the drawers are designed specifically for storage of either videocassettes or compact disks.

The 81/2-inch-wide drawers in 6A–D will hold eighteen videocassettes in three optional compartments (Figure 9.3). Make the dividers out of 1/4-inch plywood and set them into dadoes cut 1/4 inch deep in the sides.

The 161/4-inch-wide drawers in cabinets 6E–H will hold thirty-six videocassettes in six compartments, as shown in Figure 9.4. A similar drawer made 14 inches from front to back instead of 20 and installed in side cabinet 7C will hold twenty-four cassettes in four compartments.

Figure 9.5 shows how the same 161/4-inch-wide drawer made 2 inches deeper can house compact disks. Made 20 inches from front to back, it will fit the deeper of the side cabinets, as illustrated in 7D, and will hold 135 CD jewel cases in nine compartments. A drawer 14 inches front to back will fit the shallower cabinets (161/2 inches deep) and hold ninety compact disks in six compartments.

Compare the drawer configurations in 7C and 7D. In 7C the upper drawer cavity will accommodate a drawer deep enough to hold videocassettes only. However, you can replace the deeper, lower drawer with a drawer built to hold compact disks. In 7D, the drawer cavities are the same and will

hold a pair of CD drawers. Likewise, you can install one or two drawers configured to hold videocassettes. What's more, the drawer arrangement illustrated in 7C can be applied to 7D and vice versa.

If you've planned for plenty of cassette storage in the side cabinets, consider leaving out the cassette drawer to the left of the VCR shelf in the television cabinet. Use the space to house another audio or visual component. The partition in cabinets 6A–D can be centered for this purpose, leaving space enough for most components.

If you have a lot of compact disks and videocassettes, you may need more storage space than the standard plans allow. In this case, you can alter the side cabinets. It's an easy matter to replace their adjustable shelving with drawers. These drawers need not have applied fronts (although they could); they can instead be concealed behind a solid door. The drawers can be positioned anywhere within the available range of space. Because the drawers have a built-in finger hold at the bottom of each front end, no additional pulls are needed. Figure 9.6 illustrates additional drawers installed in cabinet 7A.

## Knobs and Pulls

The finishing touch to doors and drawers is the application of knobs or pulls. This is so much a matter of personal taste that suggestions on which kind to use would be irrelevant. A few words on the placement of hardware might be helpful, however. As a matter of symmetry, knobs and pulls are centered on a drawer front. It's not very often you see a drawer handle off center. And it's not very often you see a door handle right in the middle of the door. Handles are nearly always placed along the edge opposite the hinges and off center up and down as well. Which direction up or down will depend on whether the door is high or low in the cabinet. Place the handle in the upper (or lower) third of the door but at least 2

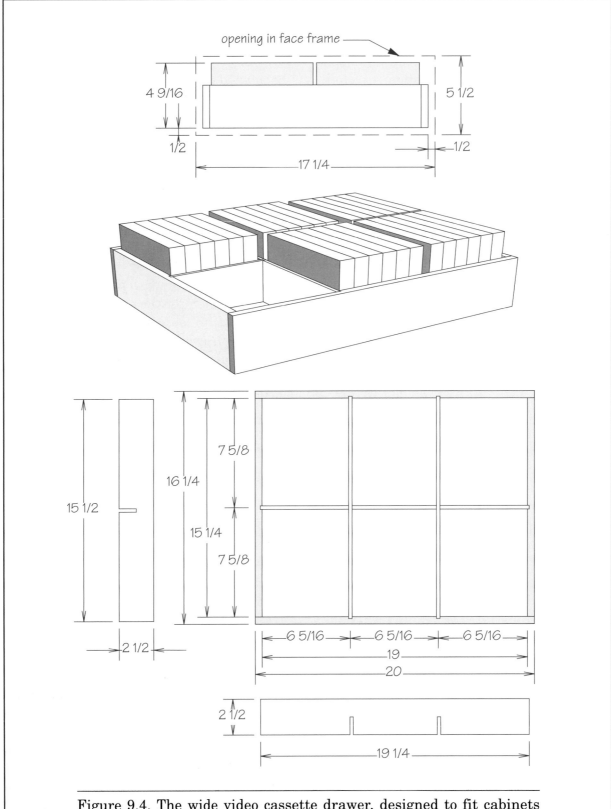

Figure 9.4. The wide video cassette drawer, designed to fit cabinets 6E–H, holds thirty-six cassettes. It will also fit into cabinets 7B and 7D. A drawer 14 inches deep instead of 20 will fit into cabinets 7A and 7C.

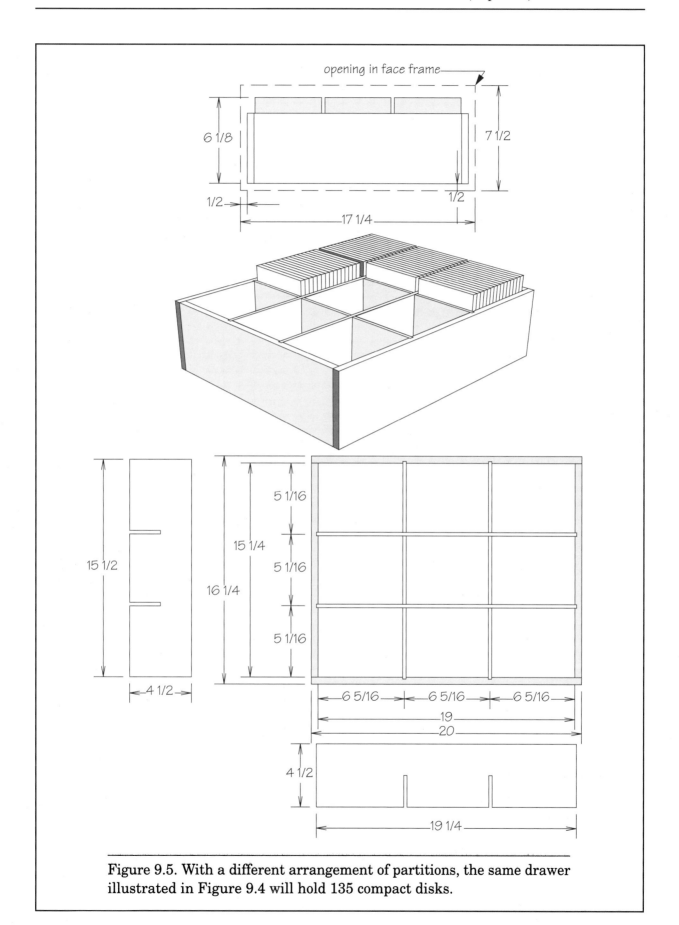

**Figure 9.5. With a different arrangement of partitions, the same drawer illustrated in Figure 9.4 will hold 135 compact disks.**

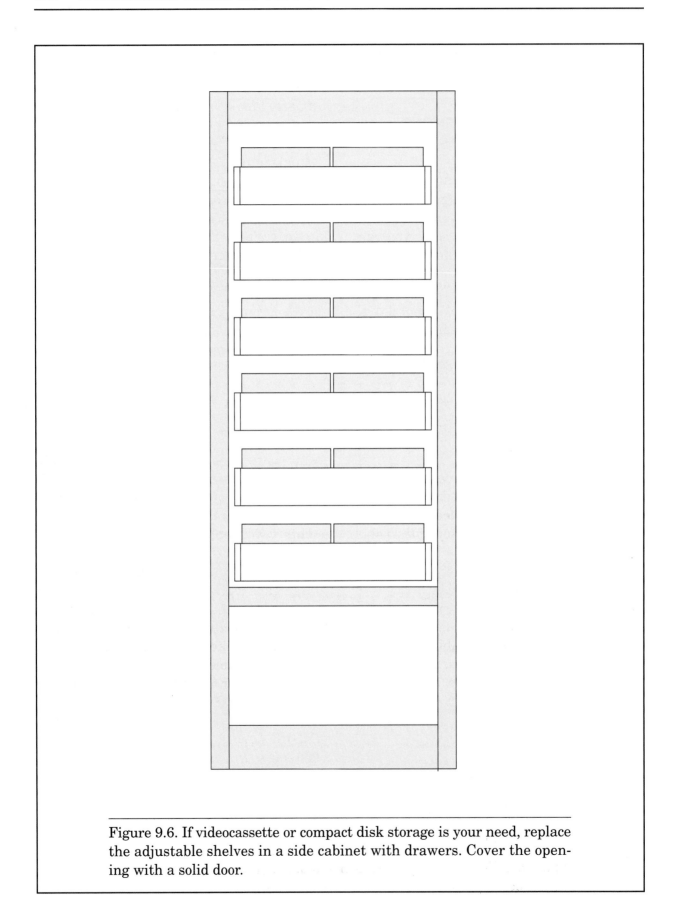

Figure 9.6. If videocassette or compact disk storage is your need, replace the adjustable shelves in a side cabinet with drawers. Cover the opening with a solid door.

inches from the corner. Before drilling any holes, try two or three positions to see which one suits best.

## ADJUSTABLE AND SUSPENDED SHELVES FOR THE TELEVISION CABINETS

If you're using a television unit that is 72 or 76 inches tall, you can give it more versatility by replacing the fixed shelf with one or two adjustable shelves. Or you can install a fixed, suspended shelf in any of the units.

Adding an adjustable shelf (discussed in chapter 3) precludes the use of flipper doors, as there is no fixed shelf to define the vertical dimension of the doors.

Figure 9.7 shows front and side sections of cabinet 6C with a suspended-shelf unit. A suspended shelf is ideal for a center speaker (used in a home-theater setup), VCR, or other component. Because the sides of the shelf are set in from the cabinet sides, flipper doors can be installed covering the full height of the television cavity. The shelf unit can be made to any size, limited only by the top of the television and the top of the cabinet. What's more, adjustable or fixed shelves can be added to the unit for extra space (figure 9.7 shows an adjustable shelf).

Use four to six 1¼-inch screws or size 10 biscuits to join the shelf to the sides. Suspend the unit from the cabinet top with four 1½-inch angle brackets, mounted on either the inside or outside of the unit, whichever is more convenient.

## ARCHES, SCROLLS, AND ROUTER WORK

An interesting way to add style to your entertainment center is to cut an arch or other scrollwork into one or more of the rails. Figure 9.8 gives examples.

These features would likely be used in cavities without doors. Flush or overlay doors, however, can be made to correspond to an arch or other simple shape, if you're willing to put in the time. Also, you could use frameless doors of plate glass (arched or square) over such fancy work.

Chamfering or rounding over the edges of the face frame with a router will also add visual interest to the piece. There are dozens of bit sizes and patterns to choose from, and your best guide is your local woodworking store or a catalog. Keep in mind, however, that a little router work goes a long way, and it's easy to overdo it. Unless you are striving for an elaborate style, simple is better. Before doing any router work, make several test cuts on pieces of waste stock large enough for you to get a good idea of what a given cut would look like on the finished piece.

## COMBINING THE UNITS INTO ONE PIECE

Once completed, the individual units of your entertainment center can remain unattached to one another. Indeed, this is how most, if not all, store-bought sectional entertainment centers are sold. This presents two problems, however. First, any unevenness in the floor will be transmitted to the top of the units, which could result in large gaps if the individual units lean one way or another. The second problem is how to go about adding trim around the top and bottom to make the pieces appear as an integrated whole.

The answer to both problems is to fasten them together. You could use screws or nuts and bolts. A better way is to use knock-down (KD) fasteners. Unlike nuts or bolts, KD fasteners are inconspicuous, and unlike screws, they can be taken apart and reassembled an indefinite number of times and still maintain exact alignment. There are several different brands and kinds of KD fasteners for different jobs, but the type that applies to entertainment centers is shown in Figure 9.9.

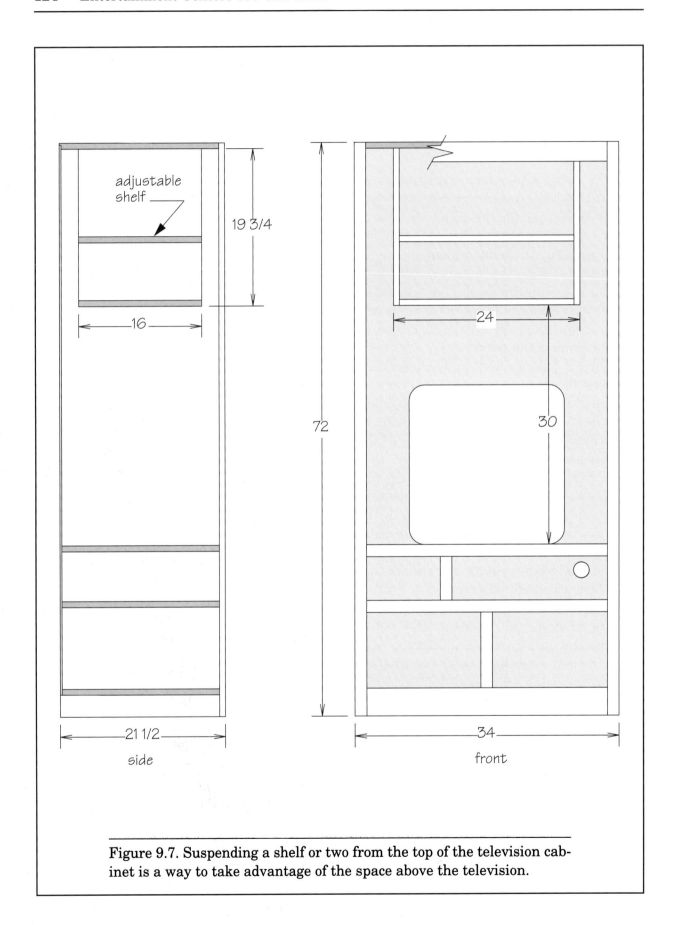

Figure 9.7. Suspending a shelf or two from the top of the television cabinet is a way to take advantage of the space above the television.

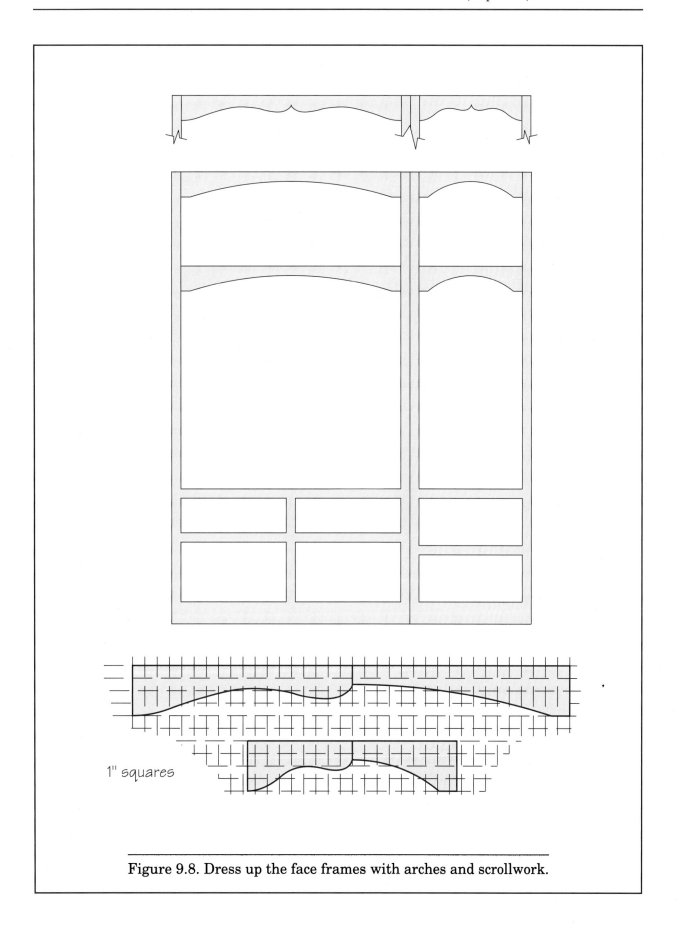

Figure 9.8. Dress up the face frames with arches and scrollwork.

1" squares

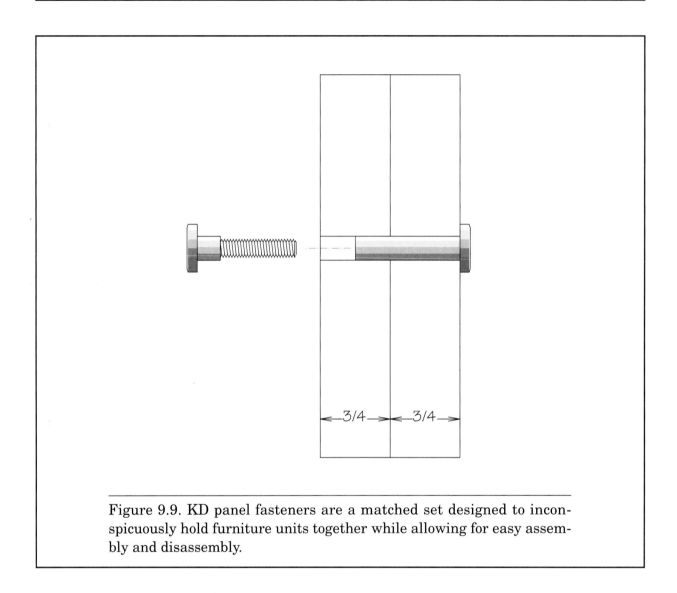

Figure 9.9. KD panel fasteners are a matched set designed to inconspicuously hold furniture units together while allowing for easy assembly and disassembly.

To install the fasteners for the first time, clamp the units together, lay out their positions—two at the top and two at the bottom—and bore the specified diameter hole for that brand through both cabinets. Don't forget to use a backing block on the exit side of the bore.

Once the units are bolted together, you can cut and install trim for the top and bottom and ensure that the pieces will be in perfect alignment.

## TRIMMING THE BOTTOM AND TOP

Adding crown molding at the top and an apron at the bottom is another way to vary the style of your entertainment center. Both are done best when the individual units are bolted together (see above).

### Apron

An apron will protect the bottom edges of the entertainment center as well as add visual bulk to the base. An apron can be cut from a suitable off-the-shelf molding, or you can make it yourself from 3/4-inch stock. The simplest apron has a rounded or chamfered top edge (Figure 9.10). Of course you can use beads and other designs to dress up the apron. When making the apron stock, remember to allow for door and drawer clearance.

Another way to dress up an apron is to cut an arch or scallop in the front piece, as shown in Figure 9.11. The bottom rail of the face frame will need to be cut away for this procedure, and you are limited in height by the bottom shelf and other blocking. This is, of course, assuming that you keep the apron flush with the bottom of the face frame. It's a simple matter, however, to make a taller apron by extending it beyond the bottom of the cabinet, but you will need to reinforce the corners. If you do add to the height of the cabinet by making the apron taller, don't

forget to consider the impact this will have on adding casters or levelers. Note that you will have to add any reinforcement and backing to the bottom of the cabinet before bolting the pieces together.

If the design of your entertainment center calls for the television cabinet and the side cabinets to be flush across the face, only two outside miter cuts are required, one on each of the right and left side cabinets. The other ends of the apron are cut square and flush with the sides of the individual cabinets.

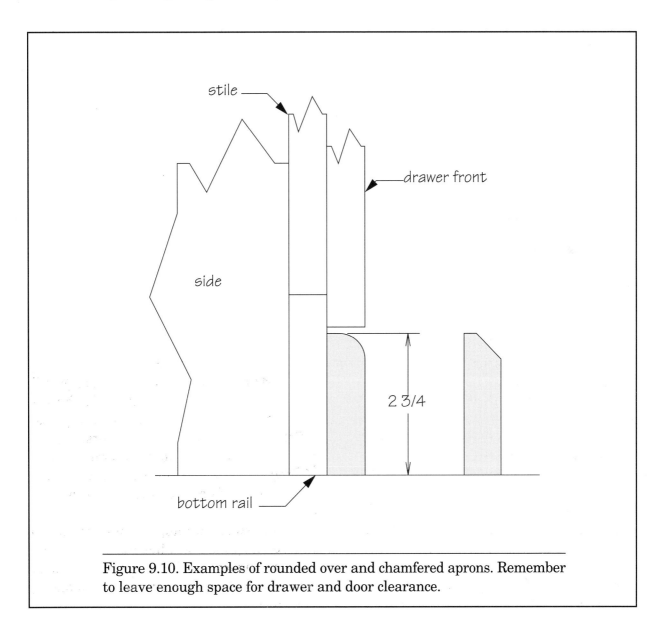

Figure 9.10. Examples of rounded over and chamfered aprons. Remember to leave enough space for drawer and door clearance.

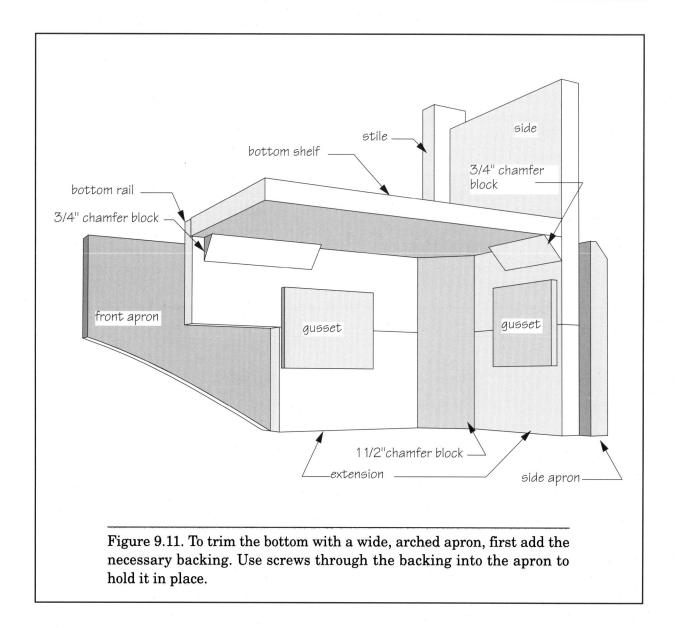

Figure 9.11. To trim the bottom with a wide, arched apron, first add the necessary backing. Use screws through the backing into the apron to hold it in place.

## Crown

Crown molding covers the plywood edges and ties the tops of the components together. It also has a great effect on the style and personality of the finished piece. Adding crown molding to the top is a similar procedure to adding an apron at the bottom, as far as miters and offsets are concerned. And like the apron, you can use off-the-shelf items or make your own molding.

There are many ways to dress up the top of your entertainment center. Figure 9.12A shows a simple cove molding flush with the top surface of the cabinet. Figure 9.12B shows a simple valance, which adds height and creates a recess perfect for the placement of low-voltage accent lights. Figure 9.12C illustrates a more elaborate crown built up of several pieces. This not only adds height but lends a feeling of massiveness to the piece.

These two latter approaches are recommended only for the taller units where the person of average height will not be able to see the top of the cabinet once the molding is in place.

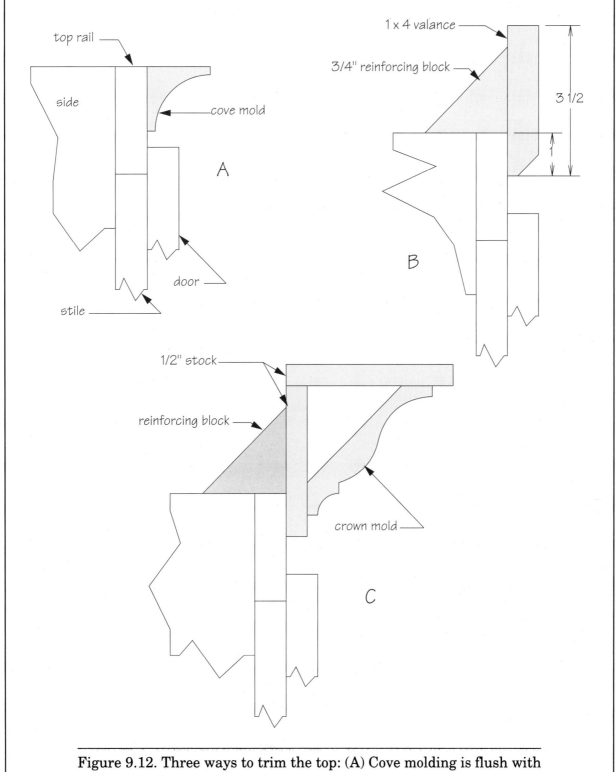

top rail

side

cove mold

A

door

stile

1 x 4 valance

3/4" reinforcing block

3 1/2

B

1/2" stock

reinforcing block

crown mold

C

Figure 9.12. Three ways to trim the top: (A) Cove molding is flush with the top. (B) A simple valance adds height or conceals light fixtures. Use reinforcing blocks at the corners and ends, and at the midpoint of the television cabinet. (C) A built-up valance adds a sense of massiveness.

# ▪ Appendix ▪

## RESOURCES FOR WOODWORKERS

Constantine's
2050 Eastchester Road
Bronx, NY 10461
Voice: 800-223-8087
Fax: 800-253-WOOD (253-9663)
Email: GRD99WDDOC@aol.com

The Candy Store for Woodworkers
7017 East New Market–Ellwood Road
Hurlock, MD 21643
800-287-4012
http://www.woodmatters.com/

The Woodworkers' Store
4365 Willow Drive
Medina, MN 55340-9701
Voice: 800-279-4441
Fax: 612-478-8395
http://woodworkerstore.com/ww/
Stores located across the United States

Woodcraft
Customer Service Dept.
P.O. Box 1686
Parkersburg, WV 26102-1686
800-535-4482
http://www.woodcraft.com/
Stores located across the United States

For a comprehensive on-line listing of
hundreds of resources for woodworkers:
The Woodworking Catalog
http://www.woodworking.com/

# ▪ Metric Conversions ▪

## INCHES TO MILLIMETERS

| IN. | MM | IN. | MM | IN. | MM | IN. | MM |
|---|---|---|---|---|---|---|---|
| 1 | 25.4 | 26 | 660.4 | 51 | 1295.4 | 76 | 1930.4 |
| 2 | 50.8 | 27 | 685.8 | 52 | 1320.8 | 77 | 1955.8 |
| 3 | 76.2 | 28 | 711.2 | 53 | 1346.2 | 78 | 1981.2 |
| 4 | 101.6 | 29 | 736.6 | 54 | 1371.6 | 79 | 2006.6 |
| 5 | 127.0 | 30 | 762.0 | 55 | 1397.0 | 80 | 2032.0 |
| 6 | 152.4 | 31 | 787.4 | 56 | 1422.4 | 81 | 2057.4 |
| 7 | 177.8 | 32 | 812.8 | 57 | 1447.8 | 82 | 2082.8 |
| 8 | 203.2 | 33 | 838.2 | 58 | 1473.2 | 83 | 2108.2 |
| 9 | 228.6 | 34 | 863.6 | 59 | 1498.6 | 84 | 2133.6 |
| 10 | 254.0 | 35 | 889.0 | 60 | 1524.0 | 85 | 2159.0 |
| 11 | 279.4 | 36 | 914.4 | 61 | 1549.4 | 86 | 2184.4 |
| 12 | 304.8 | 37 | 939.8 | 62 | 1574.8 | 87 | 2209.8 |
| 13 | 330.2 | 38 | 965.2 | 63 | 1600.2 | 88 | 2235.2 |
| 14 | 355.6 | 39 | 990.6 | 64 | 1625.6 | 89 | 2260.6 |
| 15 | 381.0 | 40 | 1016.0 | 65 | 1651.0 | 90 | 2286.0 |
| 16 | 406.4 | 41 | 1041.4 | 66 | 1676.4 | 91 | 2311.4 |
| 17 | 431.8 | 42 | 1066.8 | 67 | 1701.8 | 92 | 2336.8 |
| 18 | 457.2 | 43 | 1092.2 | 68 | 1727.2 | 93 | 2362.2 |
| 19 | 482.6 | 44 | 1117.6 | 69 | 1752.6 | 94 | 2387.6 |
| 20 | 508.0 | 45 | 1143.0 | 70 | 1778.0 | 95 | 2413.0 |
| 21 | 533.4 | 46 | 1168.4 | 71 | 1803.4 | 96 | 2438.4 |
| 22 | 558.8 | 47 | 1193.8 | 72 | 1828.8 | 97 | 2463.8 |
| 23 | 584.2 | 48 | 1219.2 | 73 | 1854.2 | 98 | 2489.2 |
| 24 | 609.6 | 49 | 1244.6 | 74 | 1879.6 | 99 | 2514.6 |
| 25 | 635.0 | 50 | 1270.0 | 75 | 1905.0 | 100 | 2540.0 |

The above table is exact on the basis: 1 in. = 25.4 mm

### U.S. TO METRIC
1 inch = 2.540 centimeters
1 foot = .305 meter
1 yard = .914 meter
1 mile = 1.609 kilometers

### METRIC TO U.S.
1 millimeter = .039 inch
1 centimeter = .394 inch
1 meter = 3.281 feet or 1.094 yards
1 kilometer = .621 mile

**INCH–METRIC EQUIVALENTS**

| FRACTION | DECIMAL EQUIVALENT | | FRACTION | DECIMAL EQUIVALENT | |
| | CUSTOMARY (IN.) | METRIC (MM) | | CUSTOMARY (IN.) | METRIC (MM) |
| --- | --- | --- | --- | --- | --- |
| 1/64 | .015 | 0.3969 | 33/64 | .515 | 13.0969 |
| 1/32 | .031 | 0.7938 | 17/32 | .531 | 13.4938 |
| 3/64 | .046 | 1.1906 | 35/64 | .546 | 13.8906 |
| 1/16 | .062 | 1.5875 | 9/16 | .562 | 14.2875 |
| 5/64 | .078 | 1.9844 | 37/64 | .578 | 14.6844 |
| 3/32 | .093 | 2.3813 | 19/32 | .593 | 15.0813 |
| 7/64 | .109 | 2.7781 | 39/64 | .609 | 15.4781 |
| 1/8 | .125 | 3.1750 | 5/8 | .625 | 15.8750 |
| 9/64 | .140 | 3.5719 | 41/64 | .640 | 16.2719 |
| 5/32 | .156 | 3.9688 | 21/32 | .656 | 16.6688 |
| 11/64 | .171 | 4.3656 | 43/64 | .671 | 17.0656 |
| 3/16 | .187 | 4.7625 | 11/16 | .687 | 17.4625 |
| 13/64 | .203 | 5.1594 | 45/64 | .703 | 17.8594 |
| 7/32 | .218 | 5.5563 | 23/32 | .718 | 18.2563 |
| 15/64 | .234 | 5.9531 | 47/64 | .734 | 18.6531 |
| 1/4 | .250 | 6.3500 | 3/4 | .750 | 19.0500 |
| 17/64 | .265 | 6.7469 | 49/64 | .765 | 19.4469 |
| 9/32 | .281 | 7.1438 | 25/32 | .781 | 19.8438 |
| 19/64 | .296 | 7.5406 | 51/64 | .796 | 20.2406 |
| 5/16 | .312 | 7.9375 | 13/16 | .812 | 20.6375 |
| 21/64 | .328 | 8.3384 | 53/64 | .828 | 21.0344 |
| 11/32 | .343 | 8.7313 | 27/32 | .843 | 21.4313 |
| 23/64 | .359 | 9.1281 | 55/64 | .859 | 21.8281 |
| 3/8 | .375 | 9.5250 | 7/8 | .875 | 22.2250 |
| 25/64 | .390 | 9.9219 | 57/64 | .890 | 22.6219 |
| 13/32 | .406 | 10.3188 | 29/32 | .906 | 23.0188 |
| 27/64 | .421 | 10.7156 | 59/64 | .921 | 23.4156 |
| 7/16 | .437 | 11.1125 | 15/16 | .937 | 23.8125 |
| 29/64 | .453 | 11.5094 | 61/64 | .953 | 24.2094 |
| 15/32 | .468 | 11.9063 | 31/32 | .968 | 24.6063 |
| 31/64 | .484 | 12.3031 | 63/64 | .984 | 25.0031 |
| 1/2 | .500 | 12.7000 | 1 | 1.000 | 25.4000 |